I DIE
EACH
TIME I
HEAR
THE
SOUND

ALSO BY MIKE DOUGHTY:

Slanky: Poems

The Book of Drugs: A Memoir

I DIE
EACH
TIME I
HEAR
THE
SOUND

BY

MIKE DOUGHTY

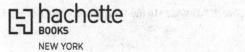

NEW YORK

Hachette Books
Hachette Book Group
1290 Avenue of the Americas
New York, NY 10104
hachettebookgroup.com
twitter.com/hachettebooks
Instagram.com/hachettebooks

First Edition: November 2020

Hachette Books is a division of Hachette Book Group, Inc.

The Hachette Books name and logo are trademarks of Hachette Book Group, Inc.

The publisher is not responsible for websites (or their content) that are not owned by
the publisher.

The Hachette Speakers Bureau provides a wide range of authors for speaking events.
To find out more, go to www.hachettespeakersbureau.com or call (866) 376-6591.

Print book interior design by Jeff Williams.

Library of Congress Cataloging-in-Publication Data

Names: Doughty, Mike, author.
Title: I die each time I hear the sound / Mike Doughty.
Description: First edition. | New York: Hachette Books, 2020.
Identifiers: LCCN 2020028316 | ISBN 9780306825316 (paperback) | ISBN
9780306825323 (ebook)
Subjects: LCSH: Doughty, Mike—Anecdotes. | Rock musicians—United
States—Anecdotes.
Classification: LCC ML420.D737 A3 2020 | DDC 782.42166092 [B]—dc23

LC record available at https://lccn.loc.gov/2020028316

ISBNs: 9780306825316 (trade paperback); 9780306825323 (ebook)

For K.R.D.: I miss you.

CONTENTS

GHOST OF VROOM

Before I wrote this, I recorded an album called *Ghost of Vroom*. It was a working title for a Soul Coughing album; in 1994, I wanted to call our first album *Ruby Vroom* so we could follow up with the dub version: *Ghost of Vroom*.

It's a play on *Garvey's Ghost*, a dub version of Burning Spear's 1976 album *Marcus Garvey*.

After I moved from New York to Memphis, I became less interested in my acoustic thing—I spent three years writing songs that sound like Soul Coughing: that mixture of Tom Waits and A Tribe Called Quest. I put up lo-fi recordings online. I wrote two hundred songs.

The title signifies *what if.*

Andrew "Scrap" Livingston plays bass—actually a cello, but functionally an upright bass—and Gene Coye plays drums; we didn't make him use a click track, so he could subtly manipulate how time moves. I play the sampler: Not loops arranged with a sequencer, but buttons that trigger noises. Like a Mellotron or a sound-effects machine.

The producer is Mario Caldato Jr., whose fan I became when he did the Beastie Boys' *Check Your Head*. Working with him is another planned step untaken in 1994. We did it at his house in Eagle Rock, in Los Angeles—it smelled, as all great studios do, of smoldering vacuum tubes—and we recorded fast, to outrun second-guesses.

While we were mixing, Mario looked up and said in his supernaturally mellow tone, "This is the only record that sounds like this." Like he was trying to process it.

1

The next day, he said again, "There aren't any other records that sound like this."

He started saying it often—first in puzzlement, then with conviction.

Instead of *What Would Jesus Do?* we were going with WWNED: *What Would Nobody Else Do?*

I'd tried to get Soul Coughing back together to do it. At least so I could say I took a shot. But old weirdnesses die hard. My manager said something about making sure songs were ready before we went in—we'd be doing it on our own dime. One of my ex-bandmates replied—this is 100 percent real—"Soul Coughing had no songs. We were masters of illusion."

So, *Ghost of Vroom* it is.

Hey, also: I wrote another book.

DISCLAIMER? NO/YES

My editor Ben asked me to write this book. I didn't want to.

I'd learned on the first book that subjectivity is terror.

I don't trust my stories; I don't trust my mind.

It would be impolite to say no, though, so instead I asked for too much money. Ben gave it to me. I spent the money.

So now I write a book.

I'm doing what I did last time, but with rueful awareness: I'm writing what I remember as I remember it.

Before my first book came out, I sat down with people to warn them. I met _____ in a triangular park in the West Village—a traffic island in Eighth Avenue, near where we used to live. We drank iced coffee from a bodega.

"Of course, you must've written about when *a* was *b* and we went to *c*," she said.

What happened? She told me the story: a great story.

I told her I wished I'd remembered it—and put it in the book.

I told her one of the stories I'd included. She didn't remember it.

Twenty-five years before, we'd get this one friend of ours high and passive-aggressively imprison her: she'd crash on the couch; every morning we'd beg her to stay.

She'd moved to Cleveland, had a kid, got a degree as a speech therapist. She discovered that special-ed kids loved Biggie Smalls and knock-knock jokes.

She came to a gig at the Beachland. I told her the stories that _____ and I had traded—how funny it was that we remembered completely different ones.

She didn't remember *any* of them.

"I was shocked that you didn't mention the time when *x* did *y* at the *z*," she said.

I didn't remember that.

ABSOLUTELY NEW

In 1963, John Cage organized a performance of Erik Satie's *Vexations*. The written score covers just half a page; Satie meant for it to be repeated 840 times.

Above the piece, Satie wrote, "It would be advisable to prepare oneself beforehand, in the deepest silence, by serious immobilities."

The performance, at a disused vaudeville theater, took eighteen hours, played by a rotating crew of ten pianists, among them John Cale—who would later cofound the Velvet Underground—and the choreographer Viola Farber.

Tickets were five bucks. Only one person watched the entire performance. When it was over, somebody yelled, "Encore!"

Afterward, Cage drove to his house outside the city. He slept twelve hours.

"When I got up, the world looked new," Cage wrote later. "Absolutely new."

WHOLE (2002)

My friend Pat Dillett, the record producer, had a spare ticket for an early-evening benefit: Ray Charles was playing at the Museum of Natural History. This was a few years before the Jamie Foxx movie and the reverence at the end of Ray's life.

Pat's wife was the museum's lawyer. Counsel for the bones.

I met Pat outside the planetarium. He told me that when he met his wife for lunch on a weekday, she'd ask incredulously who these people were, walking around the world, not at work. They were us.

Chevy Chase was at the reception. Pat said, "Why is Chevy Chase here?"

We were ten feet from him; it's a weird thing to say when you're standing ten feet from somebody.

Chevy Chase made a speech about how the celebrated *Saturday Night Live* Land-Shark sketch was written at the museum in the late 1970s. Young people have taken LSD at the Museum of Natural History since LSD was invented. Not that Chevy was explicit.

In the auditorium, three men in tuxedos came onstage. They doodled instrumentals. Two had mullets. The guitars looked like the acrylic-painted instruments in a Sears catalog circa 1988.

A hype man led Ray out. He'd done this hundreds of times; he seemed to be operating at half-power.

"You are about to be! Entertained! By the genius! Ray Charles!" he said.

He listed awards and million-sellers, and seated Ray at a keyboard.

The trio jumped into a smooth-jazz replica of "Hit the Road Jack." Ray had a scowl of impatience—maybe scanning for his entrance.

Then his right hand went *bink!* on a key.

A cheesy bell sound—the ideal of the digital piano. I remember Pat and me turning to each other in dread, but that can't be—it was milliseconds before the next note.

Ray rocked the hell out of that cheesy sound.

Every phrase was shocking, then inevitable. The music stretched time, which transformed into space. There wasn't a sense of *Oh, here's a guy messing around with structures.* It was contemplative, in the sense that implies interiority.

He played "What'd I Say" but didn't bother to sing.

A cloudy exploration rolled off the stage—arrhythmic and eerie. The band looking exactly like they were playing a cocktail function, Ray in supernatural speculation but somehow looking like he wasn't working that hard.

The chords parted; from nowhere Ray sang, *The whole day through.*

"Georgia on My Mind" from nothingness.

Ray sang from then on—the songs but not the songs.

He held his wrist to his ear and frowned. I thought, *How poetic: listening to his watch tick!*

Then I realized: Ray's blind. He's wearing a talking watch.

The listless hype man came to lead him offstage. "You! Have been! Entertained! By the genius! Ray Charles!"

I thought of the Land Shark, and how hallucinogens do to music what music is supposed to do to itself.

The trio briskly buttoned up the tune. They stopped; restrained applause.

The audience murmured, gathering jackets.

Now we'd returned to time: normal time. Terrifying.

The world was absolutely new.

HORN, SOOT (1991)

_____ and I stayed up all night and impulsively took the 4:30 a.m. train to her mother's house in New Canaan.

The Metro-North terminates there; at dawn, we walked from the platform into the empty town of meticulously-picturesque streets. Closed stores displayed the kind of turquoise-sphere bracelets that Linda Evans wore on *Dynasty*.

In the afternoon, I woke up and realized I had to work in Manhattan that night.

I got a ride to the city from her brother. He had a diesel station wagon—blue like the Swedish flag. There wasn't much room: it was crammed with his friends and their guitars. Nice guitars, bought with money from summer jobs, which their parents had obliged them to get as lessons in self-reliance.

They argued, as we drove, about blues-guitar authenticities.

We stopped at a mall in Stamford, the one from *Scenes from a Mall*, with Woody Allen and Bette Midler: a mall that *really* looked like a mall.

I went to Sam Goody looking for A Tribe Called Quest. I'd seen "Jazz (We've Got)" on Ralph McDaniels's *Video Music Box*. It has a trumpet sample that sounds like a mermaid skeleton floating in a lagoon.

Sam Goody was lit with dingy neon, which spilled onto the mall's clean tiles. The store's displays were for 1991's most intrusively anodyne music: Amy Grant, "Do the Bartman," the original motion-picture soundtrack of *The Bodyguard*.

Two guys were stocking CDs. One was repeating an imitation of somebody—a manager, a shoplifter?—with the catchphrase "But yeh have no pruff!"

His coworker's face suggested that the joke stopped being funny a month ago.

"Yeh have no pruff! Yeh have no pruff!" the guy kept saying.

I found a lone copy of *The Low End Theory* among the cassettes. I beat everybody else back to the parking garage to get the shotgun seat—I wanted to be next to the tape deck.

We took the Merritt Parkway, which opened in 1938, when only people with real money owned cars and a parkway was intended to be something like an actual park. The overpasses are 1930s-public-works style, like the Hoover Dam.

The closer we got to the city, the less the air smelled like trees, and the more it smelled like exhaust: summer green into charcoal gray.

I cut the cellophane wrap with a key and shoved the cassette in the tape deck.

The sound is a collage of samples of jazz and soul-jazz LPs, layered over a drum machine. Each track combines not just the sampled instruments, but those recordings' textures—characteristics that, in context, you wouldn't notice but that are audible in contrast: a bass sample isn't just the bass but the microphone used on the bass, what tape was used, how the signal was compressed, and, finally, the condition of the vinyl it was sampled from. Slight warps; abstruse patterns of crackling dust.

One of the most wonderful things about *The Low End Theory* is its surfeit of characters. The principals are Q-Tip—wry and reserved—and Phife—the chirping foil—but the cameos—Lord Jamar, Dinco D, Diamond D, many others—are essential. Each guest verse is like Robert De Niro's *twenty-seven-B-stroke-six* monologue in *Brazil*.

We passed into New York State, where there was more trash on the roadsides; trees seemed bent by soot.

The Merritt became the Hutchinson.

We went west on the Cross County, then down the Saw Mill, through the Bronx.

The green became even less green.

We passed Riverdale—houses that looked like castles.

We crossed Spuyten Duyvil Creek into Manhattan.

We drove under the George Washington Bridge.

Harlem loomed on a bluff.

We passed the white Le Corbusier rectangles on the Upper West Side.

In Midtown, the West Side Highway stopped being a highway; traffic slowed at the lights. There were still strip clubs and auto-body shops in the far West Thirties.

The ruined piers appeared on our right.

After "Scenario," featuring the legendary psychedelic-lion turn by Busta Rhymes, there was tape hiss, *clack*, and the deck shut off.

The world was absolutely new.

Can we listen to that again? I asked, stunned.

"No!" they shouted.

MINE (1992)

_____'s father bought her a studio apartment in a doorman building on Sheridan Square. She called the apartment the Universe, because a downstairs neighbor had complained about stomping, then apologized, saying, "I know I've created my own universe."

I came over to get high and stayed for a year.

We lived for *Dragnet*, which Nick at Nite showed at 2 a.m. The color episodes, from the late 1960s: detective Joe Friday reckoning with hippie kids, acid parties. Then they showed *Too Close for Comfort*: something about Ted Knight's sweaters filled us with rage. We were working our way through the nine-disc *Complete Stax/Volt Singles* box set, which _____ bought because she could afford to walk into Tower Records and spend $89.98 on a whim.

"These Arms of Mine" is track six, disc two.

When Otis Redding sang the word *mine*—the second repetition, when the note gets higher—that word *mine* became a glowing flower, which expanded into the sky, then the sky opened into the cosmos beyond the cosmos.

How corny to call singing *angelic*—what I mean is this one being, Otis, gooey and luminous, became a trillion beings, blotting out the clouds. Each being was one Otis, but also every person ever alive, all at once.

When I get migraines, like a lot of people, I see an aura: a pulsating diamond spot at the center of my vision. As it grows, it folds out like the paper fortune-tellers that girls made in fourth grade. The world becomes a dancing Fortress of Solitude.

My auras last about an hour; the word *mine* is one bar in waltz time. Three seconds?

It's also an entire August day in Fairbanks, Alaska; it's the whole of Robert De Niro's *twenty-seven-B-stroke-six* monologue in *Brazil*; it's the amount of time it takes to get a master's in philosophy and the epiphany about Heidegger, that the idea of *Geworfenheit*—or "thrown-ness" into your subjective world—is ridiculous because, come on, the guy was a Nazi.

There's a Jorge Luis Borges story, "The Aleph," written in 1945: a man finds, in a Buenos Aires basement, an object that is not an object, in which you see at a single point every possible perspective on everything that exists:

> *In that single gigantic instant I saw millions of acts both delightful and awful; not one of them occupied the same point in space, without overlapping or transparency. . . . I saw the Aleph from every point and angle, and in the Aleph I saw the earth and in the earth the Aleph.*

It's also—incredibly—a real moment in the living history of humanity that actually happened, that was recorded to a piece of tape, in Memphis, in October 1962.

The song faded out; there was disorienting silence before track seven, disc two: "Teardrop Sea" by the Tonettes.

The world was absolutely new.

JESUS ON THE CEILING (1977)

At the Wal-Mart in Leavenworth, my mom bought me a knock-off Darth Vader mask and a knockoff lightsaber—labeled, like, "space helmet" and "laser sword." I got my first migraine on the way home.

There was a *FIREWORKS!* stand that they stored behind Walmart in the winter. I looked at it and the graphic of bursting dynamite vanished—unless I looked a little bit away from it; I could see it peripherally. I looked at my hand and some of my fingers had vanished; I looked out the window and the front of the Fraternal Order of Eagles Aerie No. 55 was blankness.

Gradually the blanknesses became shimmers, grew, took over the visible world.

My mom sent me to bed. I fell asleep with the aura at full blast; woke up to excruciating pain in my skull; fell back asleep.

I woke up again. The ceiling of my room was textured stucco—I just looked it up; it was a variety called "stipple brush ceiling texture." I was between asleep and awake; the veins of stucco shifted, joined, and resolved into a vision of Jesus. His arms were outstretched—left hand gesturing to his empty tomb, his right hand to Golgotha.

SPIRIT (1991)

I took poetry classes with a woman who tended bar at the Knitting Factory. She was Jewish and hippie-goth-y—of a common 1991 style.

A week after I graduated from college, I went to meet a girl there. She ditched. It could've been a stroke of luck, as I was much more into the hippie-goth-y bartender, but I was too intimidated to ask her out.

The ceiling of the Knitting Factory was covered in a quilt of sweaters, grimy with cigarette residue, sewn together. A fire hazard only possible in pre-Giuliani New York.

The bartender was laughing with a drunk friend—only other person in the bar—who, years later, would reintroduce himself at an anniversary screening of *Wet Hot American Summer*: the director David Wain.

She mentioned that one of her coworkers flaked—they didn't even know where he was. Did I want to work that night?

I told the manager I didn't know how to make drinks. He told me to ask the customer what's in it. Like a margarita or a screwdriver, basic drinks. I had no idea. But the regulars were used to unprofessionalism.

The next week they switched me to the door. I had that job for three years.

Declining to hire a carpenter, the owner had built a towering desk, which looked like a judge's bench in a Joe Sedelmaier commercial.

From that perch, I yearned for the hippie-goth-y bartender.

Before the bar opened one night, she put on the cassette of Nirvana's *Nevermind*. I hated *college rock*, or *alternative*, or whatever you called it, because it belonged to rich kids at rich-kid schools, who played by scolding rules. The asceticism that rich kids are attracted to: they don't have to live there.

But the first song was a shock of realness: "Smells Like Teen Spirit." When it drops to just the bass, drums, and the two pinging guitar notes: rapture. The empty bar was ringing.

The world was absolutely new.

I decided to go to Tower Records and spend $9.98 on the tape, which was significant: I made $5 an hour. I wanted to listen to it the way I listened to all the songs I loved: over and over again on the F train, blasting out my ears with a Walkman.

_____ was trying to get rid of her cable, which took baffling effort: the customer service people at Time Warner couldn't believe you weren't moving, that you just wanted them to *take the box away*. For the moment she still had MTV.

I saw the video for "Smells Like Teen Spirit."

When did you hear something *good* on MTV—at least before midnight? We watched MTV just for the arty-animated bumpers between commercials, which were so great that we'd suffer through Whitesnake.

An hour later, they played the video again; again an hour later.

You could turn on MTV at any time and there would be "Smells Like Teen Spirit." I didn't need the cassette: I could count on it *just being on*. There were songs I liked on *120 Minutes*, and occasionally there'd be a good song you'd see every other day if you kept MTV on constantly, but this was an actual *big hit popular song*.

That first fortuitous time, I cranked the TV until it sputtered; after "Smells Like Teen Spirit" was Color Me Badd.

BE (1985)

A plumber fixing something in my parents' kitchen saw the cassette case of *Fables of the Reconstruction*—which I thought was called *Reconstruction of the Fables*—and told me I should listen to the Replacements. He wore the Malcolm X glasses like all hipsters wore in the mid-1980s. Where I grew up, you never saw that kind of guy—but there he was, in my house.

He told me they were playing at Maxwell's, in Hoboken. I was fifteen and had no way of getting to a bar fifty miles away. Not to mention *into* the bar.

I found the Replacements at Uncle Phil's Records and Tapes. They had a slim section in the bins marked *Punk*, which contained, I guess, anything Uncle Phil didn't have a frame of reference for: Violent Femmes, Dead Milkmen, Hoodoo Gurus. I bought records at random from that bin, not knowing what they sounded like.

Uncle Phil was a snubby, bearded man. There were autographed Mercyful Fate posters on the walls of his store, which smelled like Marlboro Lights—which still smell like worldliness to me.

I bought *Let It Be* on a football Saturday at West Point. I walked down the hill to Highland Falls, the town beyond West Point's gates. In the distance I heard marching bands and *rah-rah-rah*s of the traditional style. West Point was (is?) still in the 1950s—on an archetypal fall Saturday, with golden light and orange leaves.

I still smell the leaves, see the fall light, whenever I hear "I Will Dare." Glinting chords at the top; happy-spider mandolin at the end.

Was the record made in a humid room in August? A drafty room in January? I never looked it up. Could anybody ever not hear *Let It Be* as an autumn Saturday in a college-football town? Impossible.

I listened on a box in the kitchen; the light became more orange by the minute. Each song was particular, like the stations of the cross. It was like a drive through fascinating towns, with a stop at a Steak 'n Shake, which was the cover of Kiss's "Black Diamond" that ends side one.

There's a quality to the album that for decades I didn't realize I was hearing: a hum from amplifiers bleeding through to the tape. They couldn't—or chose not to—isolate and suppress the noise. The last song, "Answering Machine," sounds like that amorphous hum rises to drown the world.

"Answering Machine" changed my life. You could call it a ballad were it not for the distorted guitar, the anguished yelling, the wobbly sample of a Bell Telephone operator saying, *If you need help if you need help if you'd like to make a call if you need help if you'd like to make a call if you need help if you need help if you need help please hang up and try again.*

The world was absolutely new.

CURL

At Uncle Phil's Records and Tapes, I bought *Psychocandy* instead of *Meat Is Murder*—both in the *Punk* section—after reading an article in *Newsweek* about the Smiths and the Jesus and Mary Chain. The bass player of one band said he'd never had sex indoors; the other band's singer wore a broken hearing aid as an affectation. So *Psychocandy* it was.

The cat, who never left the space under the radiator, jumped on the counter and curled her body around the box in the kitchen.

She always did this with the Jesus and Mary Chain. Only that tape. Something about the frequencies.

MUSTANG (1986)

Older kids tried to teach me Police riffs and Clash riffs. This was as painful as algebra.

"Play it slow, then speed it up," they said.

I couldn't make sense of riffs played slowly. They didn't sound like themselves.

I felt physical despair when I tried to play fast. Like sizzling in the muscles. Exactly like homework, which made my hands hurt when I flipped textbook pages. A feeling I never explained to adults who yelled at me for tanking grades.

There was a kid who played the flute; he wanted to be the dude from Jethro Tull. He formed a band of kids who'd never played instruments. Somebody had picked guitar already, so I got bass. Most of the teen bassists of the 1980s had a more confident friend who got dibs on guitar. It's the secret history of the instrument.

A guy on the football team had a Fender Mustang bass. I knew him because in study hall he'd asked me what his senior quote should be—they had to turn in a form for the yearbook that day—and I sarcastically said, The answer, my friend, is blowing in the wind.

He thought that was genius. "Did you just make that up?"

He gave me the bass!

I learned something life-changing from the BBC series *Rock-school*, which was running on PBS: the new-wave *chrmmm chrmmm-chrmmm* sound—a sound I loved, though I didn't have language to identify it—was a technique called *palm muting*. It revealed a sacred mystery—and it was easy!

I chugged on the lowest string, yelping along—inventing one-string, one-note songs. I did it for hours alone in my room.

The world was absolutely new.

ADDENDUM ON
MARIO CALDATO JR. (1989)

I was a fan of his long before *Check Your Head*; he was one of the producers of Tone Lōc's "Wild Thing," which sampled Van Halen's "Jamie's Cryin'." A watershed in the history of sampling.

We cranked "Wild Thing" on the radio in the kitchen of a fast-food place in Carlisle, Pennsylvania, called the Taco Maker. A knockoff of a knockoff of Taco Bell.

We were only allowed to listen to Top 40 stations.

I worked exclusively in the back, because a customer had filled out a feedback card complaining that my jeans had holes in them.

The other guy in the back was a Lithuanian kid named K.K.

"Like K.K. Downing," he said.

OMINOUS STOMPING (1987)

I went to school in Western Massachusetts, where one town is bow ties and wicker furniture and the next looks like Alabama.

I lived in a kind of cheap ski-condo called a mod. We were in mod 5; I hung out in the goth girls' mod, mod 3, mooning over them while they listened to Nick Cave. My roommate was the first out gay dude I ever knew, a guy named Rick, whom I used to torture by opening his Bible—which he had for a theology class?—to read an endless begat sequence. It was really amusing (to me) when I was on acid.

I taped a picture of Keith Richards and Anita Pallenberg in our room; I listened to "Dead Flowers" and "Sister Morphine" a lot. I'd stolen a Howlin' Wolf tape from the school bookstore, and some tapes from the *Historia de la musica rock* compilation series, which were oddly omnipresent in dorms of the 1980s. I think a supply company for college bookstores had bought boxes of remaindered tapes in bulk—from Spain? Mexico? Paraguay? Some company that had gone bust and liquidated their inventory?

I stole a John Lee Hooker tape—having no idea what he sounded like—and was mesmerized by "Wednesday Evening Blues." The song veered in and out of time and tuning. I loved the specificity of Wednesday as a motif. I loved how the recording would drop to his voice, by itself—an eerie lament—then to repeating, tempo-flexible guitar runs, then to the sound of an ominous stomping foot.

The world was absolutely new.

BUS, CIGARETTES

A beautiful punk girl would come over to study with my roommate. She was giggly for a punk girl. Her head was shaved, except for a portion in front—a pompadour fragment, dyed magenta.

She had exquisite arms and hands, and was absolutely above my station. Eventually Rick pointed out that the only good reason for her to be hanging around so much was that she liked me. It blew my mind.

I started going to her room in the girls' dorm. Nobody cared if boys were in there or if you smoked: it was 1987. There was a mural in one of the bathrooms—a real mural, painted by a girl who lived in the dorm—of a rooster, with the motto *Any Cock'll Do*.

She listened to hardcore bands on a box—Minor Threat and Bad Brains. Bands I thought everybody *went to see*, but nobody *listened to*.

We had very quiet sex in her room. We were both seventeen. A friend of hers told me that she'd dumped a square, rich boyfriend, with whom she'd first had sex earlier that summer, and that she'd just begun to figure out why people like sex. I'd had sex for the first time three weeks before that.

Her parents were professors. She was from New York! We—and Rick and our friend Stacy—took the Adirondack Trailways bus. We got there at night.

It was New York, all New York, everywhere you looked. The sidewalks sparkled—there was some kind of glittery mineral mixed in the concrete, it literally sparkled. We sat on the grand staircase at Columbia—by the statue of the throned lady with the scepter—and smoked cigarettes. Always the cigarettes.

Her parents' apartment—they weren't there—was ramshackle and small: I was stunned that adults lived there. Warped wooden floors, walls needing paint. Plaster dust. Posters for festivals in Austria. Many ferns.

We slept in a sleeping bag on her bed. Her body had a fineness to it—with coarse hair and soft skin—which had been obscured by her punkness. I touched the dark stubble on her head; it tickled my palm.

I fell asleep feeling like I was living in a movie about what being a cool teenager was like. The traffic on Broadway at 110th Street, blocks away, sounded like the Gulf of Mexico.

We woke up in blinding sun—her parents had no curtain. We watched Ralph McDaniels's *Video Music Box*: Boogie Down Productions, Big Daddy Kane, the Juice Crew. Bands you'd never know had videos unless you lived in New York and watched—specifically—Ralph McDaniels's *Video Music Box*.

We took the subway to the East Village and ate at Yaffa, a café decorated in all-mismatch: beaded curtains, Victorian wallpaper. On the side of the building was a mural of a screaming girl wearing a brocaded officer's cap.

Stacy found a salon that looked like the one at which Michelle Pfeiffer worked in *Married to the Mob*. She got dreadlocks, which cost her $300—unthinkable money for a seventeen-year-old. The stylist used Elmer's glue and some kind of hot implement for melting.

What is more futuristic, I thought, than a white girl with dreadlocks?

New York felt like paradise, as it does in the autumn. We went to Washington Square; guys drifted near the trees selling dime bags;

sketchy dudes banged on guitars with missing strings. There were traces of gray violence at the periphery.

We met some friends of hers by the fountain—people she knew from Bronx Science. We smoked more. Somebody got a forty of Olde English. Night fell.

CAT-BUKS (1994)

I lived on Fourteenth Street and Second Avenue, across from that KFC that's been there forever, the New York Eye and Ear Infirmary, a Ukrainian junk shop filled with Sovietica. It was a three-bedroom, usually housing a dude just out of college in each bedroom and a random dude on the couch. We called it by the acronym of its phone number: CAT-BUKS.

My roommate went to NYU's graduate acting school. The undergraduate actors at NYU were hundreds of kids who, not having other plans, wanted to be famous. They took Method acting classes that were like crypto-therapy: role-play exercises, unpacking their newly ended childhoods. The graduate school, on the other hand, had elite classes of a dozen people who studied the Alexander Technique, elocution, fencing.

One of his classmates was an all-American handsome guy, wracked with anxiety. He was very funny about it. A bunch of people, after getting wasted, tried to teach him a parlor game called Who's the Psychiatrist?, but, not getting the rules, he assumed an overbearing psychiatrist character, which was one of the funniest stoned-party bits I've ever seen until it was the hands-down scariest.

Another guy—a very controlled and courteous guy—got drunk and crawled out on the ledge, five stories above the street. It was a party for the first week of the semester; this guy, having just arrived in New York, was having his wilding moment. This thing on the ledge was the most out-of-control thing he ever did—would ever do. This placid guy's name would always be appended with *You know, the guy who crawled out on the ledge.*

HBO! HBO! HBO! HBO!
HBO! HBO! HBO! HBO! (2001)

In the summer before 9/11, my ex-roommate's all-American classmate was on a cable show, one of the early prestige dramedies. In a promo, his character ejected spastic yelling while standing by a buffet. To his friends this summarized him hilariously.

CAT-BUKS had turned over, repeatedly, to a chain of roommates: one guy left to move in with his girlfriend; another guy, moving to New York, took his room; the first guy left; a friend of his came in. It may still be occupied by kids just out of college—our distant descendants.

The handsome all-American actor and my former roommate went to CAT-BUKS to buy mushrooms, with me in tow.

The guy selling mushrooms had replaced a guy with a drinking problem. His mushrooms were baked into chocolate kept in ice trays in the freezer: He cracked the tray's contents onto the counter while speaking sadly of the guy. A drug dealer pitying a drunk.

I wasn't buying mushrooms. I'd been sober for a little more than a year. I was going to shepherd my friends to a concert in Central Park and make sure they didn't wander into anything stressful.

I'd been hanging out with people who were getting high. I told myself this made them fun to go dancing with. I asked to look at the drugs when they bought them: tulip bulbs of purplish weed, suspended in clear boxes. I sat in their circle, taking the joint between my fingers and passing it.

We met a friend of theirs at a Starbucks on the Upper East Side. They went into the bathroom one after the other and ate the mushrooms.

We talked about the twelve-step meetings I was going to. My sobriety was pretty wobbly, as it would be for a while. Do I go, what, like every week?

No, like, every day, if I can.

It shocked them.

Colin Farrell walked past the Starbucks window. Their friend burst into tears.

"He's even more beautiful in real life," she sobbed.

So they were starting to be high.

We walked into Central Park. Every once in a while, somebody would start yelling something from a distance. I recognized it immediately:

"HBO! HBO! HBO! HBO! HBO! HBO! HBO! HBO!"

Soul Coughing had been on an HBO concert series in the mid-1990s, when I'd been living in Pensacola, crashing with a guy who refused to get cable or a phone. I rode my bike daily from his house to Sluggo's—the punk bar in Pensacola—and I'd hear somebody shouting from across the street, "HBO! HBO! HBO! HBO! HBO! HBO! HBO! HBO!"

The opening act in Central Park was a funk band, all of whose songs had the same template. *Baby! I want to give you love! I want to take you home!*

Or: *Girl! I want to see you dance! I want to make you happy!*

Or: *Woman! Your love's so good! I can't live without you!*

My friends got antsy, so we split before the opener finished. As we left the park, more random people in the distance shouted: "HBO! HBO! HBO! HBO! HBO! HBO! HBO! HBO!"

The name that the actor used for screen credits was peculiarly formal—along the lines of a *Washington Post* byline. He told me there had been another actor with the same name; union rules were that there could be only one.

There'd been an iconic 1980s teen star with the same name who'd also had to go with a formal-sounding variation.

He said he was having a perceptual crisis: the world was stuck in the opening act's rhythm:

Pretzels! They're a buck ninety-eight! Would you like a napkin!

And: *Hey! Can I borrow two bucks! I need to take the train!*

And: *Mom! I'm glad you called! Are you in Westchester!*

So we traded riffs:

Pants! You put them on your legs! Sometimes they're brown!

And: *Banks! They've got a bunch of bills! In the ATMs!*

And: *Coffee! It makes you awake! I find it delicious!*

From the next block: "HBO! HBO! HBO! HBO! HBO! HBO! HBO! HBO!!"

We went into Big Nick's Pizza and Burger Joint, on West Seventy-Seventh. Even then—a dozen years before it was replaced by a Bank of America—it was a dingy anachronism. It had always been.

A teen girl's eyes ballooned when we entered. When we sat down, her entire family, seven of them, shuffled up to us and wanted a picture. They were tourists from Missouri. I don't think they were fans of his show; this was the first person from television they'd ever seen.

If I sound snobby, let me make it clear that I asked for autographs from the first dozen famous people I ever met, whether I knew and liked their work or not. I still feel bad about the copious "Hang on to your dreams!" note that Eric Bogosian wrote me.

The actor grinned for the pictures—it was 2001, so these were Sony Cyber-Shots, not iPhones—but he hadn't quite learned how. He gritted his teeth. Also, he was—clearly, to me at least—living in a world of shifting color blobs.

We sat back down. The waiter said, "Drinks! Would you like to order some! Let me tell you the specials!"

PIZZA, SWORD (2007)

I did an interview with a porn site—I should say a *burlesque* site, the term then newly in vogue. It was briefly a cultural hub; they had a diligent writer who knew how to track down musicians and actors and talk them into being interviewed for a porn site. He was really good at it.

He built their brand, then died of a sudden illness.

"I'm so sick it's not even funny," he posted hours before he passed.

They gave me a membership. I chatted with some models but also met women who were just members showing off a comic-convention-sexy thing.

One woman looked like a fetchingly-chubby silent-film star: just lovely. She posted about *dinging*, which meant achieving higher character levels in *World of Warcraft*.

I replied repeatedly with the most obvious sex joke.

She was engaged; she wrote sweet tributes to her fiancé. But she betrayed a sad horniness. Inevitably, she was unengaged.

She lived in Indiana. I invited her to a Chicago show.

We sent each other texts that were just shy of *Hey, we're having sex next week*.

I looked up to the balcony during the show and thought I saw her: blue-haired, fleshy-framed. But it couldn't be her: she had her arms around a bulky guy. In a way that appeared—consoling?

The stage lights changed. I couldn't see the balcony; I squinted, seeing if she was with the guy—what she was doing with the guy?

We found each other after the show. Yes, she was with the bulky guy.

Crushing. But she was flirty? Was this not her boyfriend? This was her boyfriend.

The three of us crossed Lincoln Avenue and went to a pizza place.

She went to get slices and looked from one of us to the other and back again, in a way that was like, *You two get to know each other.*

The guy was into broadsword fighting. I want to be nice, and I'm good at asking questions. I got him talking about the choreography and, like, how heavy are those things, really?

After the pizza, they argued on the street. I decided to stop trying to figure out what was happening. I hailed a cab.

The broadsword guy was making an inaudible, petulant remark. I said, Hey, I'm just—

"No!" she said, whirling around, jabbing a finger. "Can you hold on for a moment?"

The two of us were in the cab.

I don't think I wanted to have sex, but we had sex. She was oddly pedantic about it. I'll do whatever I'm asked to do, but her instructions were irritatingly patient.

She looked at her phone afterward; she showed me a text from the broadsword guy. He apologized, and he signed off with an onomatopoetic kiss.

She said he'd insisted on the open relationship—said he just wasn't capable of monogamy. She cried. But she wanted to be with him. This policy was untested—until that night. By her.

"I am *totally* comfortable with this," she said. "He won't stay upset."

She emailed a month later: she'd realized maybe *I* wasn't totally comfortable and didn't want to sleep with somebody in an open relationship? It hadn't occurred to her.

Maybe a year after that, I looked at her page on the burlesque site. She'd married the broadsword guy.

WINNEBAGO (1978)

In Kansas, we lived half a mile from the federal prison—the notorious Leavenworth that everyone thinks of when they hear *Leavenworth*—which looks like a state capitol melded to the Death Star. Some of the prisoners were employed by a program to repopulate the plains with buffalo—at the time my family lived there, they'd just started, and there were three buffalo trotting around the prison.

The prisoners—skittish, scowling men in green jumpsuits—also worked in the grocery store: they hauled bags, plunking them into the trunk of our gargantuan Oldsmobile.

Life was in the prison's shadow; I was too young to understand how scary that was. The roller rink—classic 1970s roller-disco style—was across the street from it. We had our second-grade end-of-school-year party there. We skated to "Rock the Boat" by the Hues Corporation, and Barry Manilow's "Can't Smile Without You."

On Google Street View, I traced the route I walked from home to school, clicking my way down Cherokee Street to David Brewer Elementary School. Except for the part through Brett Friedrich's backyard, which was so vast that they needed a riding mower.

Every day we walked past a hulking Winnebago, parked in a driveway. It was still there, *forty years later*, on Street View. The green stripes had faded in the sun.

TWO QUOTES ABOUT NEW YORK

"I came to New York, an island off the coast
of America."

—SPALDING GRAY, *SWIMMING TO CAMBODIA*, 1987

"World's largest Applebee's just three blocks away"

—SIGN NAILED TO SCAFFOLDING IN TIMES SQUARE, CIRCA 2006

YOU DON'T WANT
THE OLD TIMES SQUARE (1982)

I ate a veal parmigiana at the Burger King in Times Square—yeah, Burger King really had a veal sandwich in the early 1980s. I was twelve. There was a rumor that somebody had been murdered in the bathroom.

We could see billboards for *Oh! Calcutta!* and Midori melon liqueur. My parents were going to buy cheap tickets at the TKTS booth for something on Broadway—whatever was available. We saw a production of *The Pirates of Penzance* starring Andy from *WKRP in Cincinnati*, who had replaced the original lead, Kevin Kline.

I loved the sandwich. But I don't want the old Times Square.

Visualize the corniest Pornhub banner: the font, the harshness of the pic. Imagine a livid—yet somehow tedious—shade of pink. Paint that onto ugly stores. Apply a coat of soot.

Do not visualize vintage-1970s-porn big hair and extravagantly-serifed fonts. If that seems unfair, what you want back is not Times Square, but *the 1970s*.

People remember the tracking shot of Forty-Second Street in *Midnight Cowboy*, cowboy-gigolos posing under marquees, or the tracking shot in *Taxi Driver*, with marquees reflected on the windows of Travis Bickle's car. That's the work of art directors and cinematographers.

You don't want to be in a theater sparsely populated with sketchy people jacking off. You want porn at home: I implore you to be grateful for the porn available at your extreme convenience.

The bodegas in Times Square were the best place in New York to buy fake IDs and bongs. Now weed gear is sold everywhere, and holograms have ruined the fake-ID trade. In the 1980s, your photo on a janky shard of card stock with *STUDENT* printed across the top was plenty effective.

They sold switchblades and brass knuckles in those bodegas, too—not for nothing did they have the registers behind bulletproof glass. If you want to buy those things and are not at a truck stop in Arkansas, then, yes, maybe you want the old Times Square back.

Before Disney began buying theaters and staging adaptations of, like, *Camp Rock* and *High School Musical 2*, I'd been to Shibuya Crossing in Tokyo, which everybody loved because it had the kind of giant video ads that were in *Blade Runner* and there was so much light from the billboards that the night was fake daytime.

I thought, *Why can't we have this in New York?*

Where could you put it but Times Square?

SPENCER THE INEVITABLE (1993)

I saw this guy Spencer every other time I was on lower Broadway, in the stretch between Andy's Chee-Pees and Unique Boutique. He wasn't a friend but he wasn't a not-friend. He went to school with people I went to school with.

Even if he worked near there, it wasn't like I was walking there at the same time every day. Maybe Spencer was being paid by a performance artist to walk, all day, endlessly, a route on Broadway from Wanamaker to Great Jones and back again.

Then I started seeing Spencer in other places. I saw Spencer in Boerum Hill, in Brooklyn; I saw him get off the subway at West Seventy-Ninth Street. I couldn't not see Spencer.

Initially we nodded hi; at some point, we stopped and spoke about how odd it was; after that we nodded at each other to acknowledge the oddness; then we nodded without smiling; then we gave up on acknowledging each other entirely.

Once, when I was doing bong hits at CAT-BUKS, I told everybody that I wanted somebody to invent a pair of goggles that, as you walked around New York, would display on the foreheads of passersby how many times in your life you'd seen them. Maybe the fat guy in the hard hat you'd seen twice on the subway; the kid with the lacrosse stick ten times; the lady in the caftan you'd walked by thirty-five times.

You could do that with phones, but nobody would like it.

UNIVERSAL

Universal Musical Instrument was on the part of lower Broadway where I always saw Spencer. It was on the second floor; you had to get buzzed in and walk up the stairs. It was filled with boxes of junk—old-stock drumsticks, plastic maracas, toy instruments. Magical.

Inevitably, I was the only customer.

An old Polish guy trudged out from behind the counter—a glass case, mostly empty except for a disarray of Boss pedals and used microphones. He would walk over to the guitars hanging on the wall—knockoff brands: Samick, Hondo—and, like, straighten the price tags. He was making sure I didn't shoplift.

He was nice to me once: I brought in a Fender Tele bass that'd had the frets shaved off by somebody. I traded for—an Ibanez? Something much lesser in value.

Lower Broadway changed, but it never occurred to me that Universal could be gone: it was always its own realm beyond time; wouldn't laws of nature have to bend for it to be displaced? I was there a few years ago: I was in the neighborhood and needed strings; instinctively I walked to the glass door and looked for the buzzer—baffled in spite of myself.

BRONX, RUSHING (1997)

I'd taken some E and was flopping around the hallway near the bathroom at the Blue Note, in Hoxton Square, East London. My eyes were flipping around in their sockets. I leaned into a window.

It was at Metalheadz, the Sunday evening (5 p.m.!) drum-and-bass night run by the circle of DJs adjacent to Goldie, who was the face of the genre. They spun white-label acetates procured directly from producers, tracks so new they'd never been spun.

Doc Scott spun his mighty "Shadow Boxing" for the first time, and the dance floor exploded. The ominous orchestral horns and enraged drum fills.

The world was absolutely new.

A girl was there, equally wasted, sitting in the window.

"Where are you from?" Super-thick East End accent. So sexy.

New York.

"I want to go to a party in the South Bronx," she said: *souf brunx.*

Oh yeah?

"I heard they kill you for being white," she said.

A friend of hers walked up and said, "I'm rushing! I'm rushing! I'm rushing! I'm rushing! I'm rushing! I'm rushing!"

"I want to go to the South Bronx," the girl said again.

ASTOR (1989)

A block up from Universal was Astor Place Hair; I started getting cuts there as an eighteen-year-old, when I came to the city, because it's where the cool kids from my high school went. They crossed from our side—the shifty side—of the Hudson to the posh side, where the Metro-North was. They took the train all the way to the city mostly to get haircuts that any sucker with a buzzer could do: Mohawks or rattails. Some of them got logos shaved into their head—like the Knicks or Gucci—Astor was the world capital of logo-shaving.

It was a linoleum hole, in a basement, under a vitamin store. They rented their barber chairs—beat up, with holes in the maroon vinyl held shut with tape—to itinerant cutters. Old pages clipped from *Details* and *GQ* taped to the walls.

I still associate the smell of overheated blow-dryers with the urbane.

At the bottom of a flimsy iron stairway a guy with a comb-over and a gold chain sat at a counter by a rotating fan and a bowl of Russian candies. He stared at you.

You said, "Haircut."

He swiveled leisurely, taking in the panorama of chairs; thoughtfully yelled *Ivan!* or *Pasquale!* and Ivan or Pasquale waved frenetically.

They were incompetent barbers. Each had pages ripped from magazines—movie stars—taped to their mirrors, but I doubt they could execute the styles. They had hand-written, construction-paper signs of their names—*MARCO MON TUES WEDS SAT*—surely someone had a preferred guy at Astor.

A guy by the door sold bootleg mixtapes, the DJs' names on photocopied covers. Techno, salsa, house, hip-hop, Latin freestyle.

Is it still there? Astor got to 1991 and stopped. Last time I was there, the mixtape guy was gone, but his music wasn't—they blasted old diva-house music. Among the Polaroids of freshly-trimmed celebrities in the foyer, Marky Mark and Darryl Strawberry took pride of place.

SILVER (2014)

On Instagram, I followed a woman doing Edie Sedgwick's look: she wore pharaoh makeup and dresses of fulgurating silver; she draped herself on sculptures in a park.

I commented: face with heart eyes.

The next time I looked at my phone, she'd liked twenty posts, going back months.

She sent pictures with tasteful reveals—bare shoulder—the one side of a skirt hiked up—then in her bra—evolving in gradients to nudes.

She was emaciated. You could see her sternum's ridges.

I was repulsed. But what do you do if someone starts sending you naked pictures? You are a polite person, so you flatter them.

I was horrified by how much it turned me on that she was sending me pics from public places. Not the frightening images of her body, but the thought that she was sneaking into bathrooms to take them.

Is it my place to tell someone I think she's sick? What's the courteous way to cut this off? The best I could do was take a long time to reply with a face with heart eyes.

Eventually I couldn't live with it and I asked her to stop. I said I hoped she'd get help.

She texted: *its called crohns disease look it up!!!!! how dare you????????! why did you encourage me if you're not interested??????*

She blocked my account: a relief.

She returned months later, commenting. I didn't respond at all—
yet the comments got flirtier, and flirtier still. Then she was in my
inbox, her dress pulled up to reveal the knots of her hips.

MARQUEE (1989, 2005)

Subway fare was a buck; I never had a buck. If I wanted a slice of pizza—in addition to a pack of cigarettes, a dime bag of weed, and a one-dollar Genesee Cream Ale at Sophie's on East Fifth Street—I had to walk home. Eighty-two blocks: about four miles.

My route was up Sixth Avenue—the part with all the white corporate towers. Radio City Music Hall is wedged among them. Every night, past midnight, when the avenue was deserted, I walked under Radio City's marquee, with its antique neon font announcing *TERENCE TRENT D'ARBY 5/2 MICHAEL BOLTON 6/7 VERN GOSDIN 6/29.*

All arty kids walked great distances up and down the island of Manhattan—mostly in the opposite direction that I walked, from restaurant jobs or clothes-folding jobs uptown to shitty apartments downtown. It wasn't a statement; we were just that broke.

It didn't seem weird to leave a dive bar where the Reverb Motherfuckers were playing and march—at 3 a.m.—through an empty world-media capital of the world.

Sixteen years later, my name was on that marquee. I was opening for Barenaked Ladies; I don't know if my name was there as kindness on the part of BNL or if they always put up the opener's name.

SPACE TRAIN (1973)

I staged dramas around my toy Batman. Aquaman, Robin, and the Green Arrow were there to be scene partners. They'd lost most of their clothes. I called them *my boys*.

I was having cognitive difficulty with dialogue: Since I was the only audience, why was I doing voices aloud? Couldn't I just *think* the dialogue? But trying to keep it all inside my mind was maddeningly effortful.

When we changed houses—we lived on an army base, with housing areas arranged by rank, and when your dad got promoted your family moved—my room was boxed up by a teenage mover in a headband. I asked him whether he'd packed my boys yet. The teenager replied by asking me if I knew what Vietnam was. I did not. My dad had fought in Vietnam—before I was born—but nobody had talked to me about it. I remember being afraid of the teenager.

Batman appeared twice on Saturday mornings: as a cartoon on *Super Friends*, and in the 1960s live-action series—Cesar Romero as the Joker—which had been repurposed as kids' TV. It was somehow not cognitively challenging to see two kinds of Batman who were both Batman.

People born in this century have no frame of reference for the universality of Saturday morning cartoons: a ritual in which all American children participated, from dawn to noon every single Saturday. You could be a network partisan—ABC, CBS, NBC,

PBS, a couple local channels—or you could arrange a routine and switch around.

On my agenda between *Super Friends* and *Batman* were an animated *Planet of the Apes* (a YouTube comment called it "more closely based on the novel by Pierre Boulle") and *Hong Kong Phooey*, now consigned to obscurity by its racism.

The morning ended at the opening sequence of *Soul Train*, which was a cartoon of a train chugging through space, trailing colored plumes. After that it was just teenagers dancing, which shocked me every time. *Teenagers dancing?* After how great the space train was?

I want to write a mournful country ballad called "The Cartoons Are Over When *Soul Train* Comes On."

On a Saturday in May, I switched the TV on, and saw rows of grave men, on a dais, in suits. The only thing I knew about politics—was this *politics?*—was that Henry Kissinger was not the president. I saw him on the cover of *Newsweek* and asked my mom if he was. My assumption until then was that George Washington was the president, as he'd always been.

Surely this would end quickly; surely these men would wrap it up before *Super Friends*. But they didn't.

Given the circumstance, it wouldn't compromise my dignity to watch cartoons outside my routine. But on the next channel there were the same men in suits. They need more than one channel for this? I went to the next and it was the same. Then the channel that showed girl cartoons—I was willing to watch girl cartoons!—the men in suits. Channel thirteen—shows for babies!—the men in suits. *They're doing this even to the babies!*

They crossed the nine o'clock line, knocking off *Super Friends*. Can this go to ten o'clock? It can't.

The grave men droned on.

There weren't even commercials!

They can't go through *Batman*, can they?

In my heart, I knew they could.

In bitterness, I hoped that anyone who'd *want* to watch teenagers dancing on *Soul Train* would suffer. Then I felt awful about wishing this on them.

I turned to my dad. How long can this last?

"Probably a long time," my dad said, in a weary tone unfamiliar to me.

THEY DROVE TO WORK

I can tell you that 1973's *Super Friends* didn't have the Wonder Twins and Gleek, but Wendy, Marvin, and Wonder Dog, who are no longer considered canon.

I know that I didn't watch *Isis*—it didn't appear until 1975—nor *The Lost Saucer*—also 1975—with Ruth Buzzi and Jim Nabors: actors who lived in Los Angeles and drove their cars from their houses to the set every day.

What I wish I could know is which cartoons came on before 7 a.m. that day: those were older, and unsettling. *Courageous Cat and Minute Mouse* (1960) was okay for the theme song; sometimes *The Mighty Hercules* (1963); but never the hideous *Clutch Cargo* (1959), which superimposed film of human mouths on drawings that barely moved.

FLOAT (2004)

I played on one of the small stages at Bonnaroo. Afterward, in the artists' compound, I walked past a truck: people were climbing a ladder onto its roof.

Galactic's bass player, Bobby Mac, was on the ladder; he yanked me up. Before I knew what was happening, I was standing twenty feet above the trash-strewn grass with a bunch of people on MDMA.

I realized we were on a Mardi Gras float. I peered over the edge and saw it was a giant fiberglass head.

It was the massive head of Mr. T.

The gate separating the backstage world from the ticket-holders' world opened—lugubriously—the truck rumbled, and the giant head sailed through.

We rolled onto the field in front of the main stage, at the heels of people filing toward the beer tents. Onlookers stood on a distant rise, squinting.

I found myself next to a woman with whom I'd been on a couple of dates—the sort of dates where you can't figure out whether or not you find the person attractive. She was reaching into a bin tucked under the Mohawk, pulling up strings of beads by the fistful. She hung them on my arms.

"Don't let other people take the good beads!"

My arms got heavy with beads, like wizard sleeves. A guy in a vintage Oilers shirt turned to me and said, in a tone suggesting he would not stoop to being an asshole to an asshole, "Do you mind sharing your beads?"

I have a voice in my head that punishes me for social missteps, and one of its regular accusations is *You bead hog!*

The float crawled. The driver honked at ambling clumps of people who turned around to see a massive Mr. T. head at their heels.

We wobbled up a dirt track, cruised through a sea of tents; we could hear tents being zipped open. People rushed toward the glaring face of Mr. T.

We sailed past the pulsing rave tent.

We passed a cop on a horse. The horse freaked out, twitching and whinnying. A terrified circle shrank away from it.

The giant head at last arrived at the epicenter of Bonnaroo, and stopped; we were at the edge of the late-night Buckethead set.

A hundred yards away, Buckethead was peering out, where he must've seen the silhouette of something that looked like—a big skull on wheels? Boulder? Rapa Nui monolith?

I'd been standing near a middle-aged woman in a powder-blue prom dress. Her hair was permed like Eric Clapton's in 1967. There was a smaller person standing next to her, an oddly intense little guy—something wrong with this guy?—with a goofy smile. He wore a Hawaiian shirt tucked into pleated trousers.

It was William Hung.

William Hung was the celebrated public fool of 2004. On *American Idol*, he'd sung Ricky Martin's "She Bangs" while thrashing jiggly arms. He was so uncannily inept that the word *inept* is inapt.

Was he in on the joke by now? So painful to contemplate. He must've been getting majorly paid to appear. I learned later that the woman in the powder-blue dress was his mother—his manager.

William Hung was handed a mic; he sang "She Bangs" to a karaoke track. Then he sang "Achy Breaky Heart" and "We Are the Champions."

Next to the crushing sound of Buckethead, it was barely audible (where were the speakers?). There was no spotlight on William Hung. The people on the float were hugging and throwing beads.

Did anyone dancing around the giant head know he was there? Was I alone experiencing the great sadness of William Hung? Was William Hung sad? Did the world's jokes about William Hung make William Hung's mother sad? They didn't look sad.

Could Buckethead see William Hung, flailing and hollering, surrounded by bead throwers, on the giant head of Mr. T?

CHAIR (1997, 2001)

One of my roommate's acting-school classmates was in a minor, ridiculous Shakespeare play that's revived periodically, just so people can talk about how it's so weird that Shakespeare wrote something ridiculous.

This actor was phenomenal.

I met him at one of my roommate's shows. He had a small dog, and was with a woman whom I took to be his assistant. The actor handed her the dog and told her to walk him.

He was a big fan, actually. He and a film-director friend had followed Soul Coughing shows around the Northeast the way kids followed the Dead.

They'd made a movie and wanted a Soul Coughing song in it.

The producers wouldn't let a VHS tape get into the world, so I went up to a lawyer's office and watched it in a conference room.

I met my roommate and him at a bar. His assistant was there. She got extremely close to me while we were talking. The actor had his back turned to us the whole time. With every drink, the assistant came closer.

She gave me her number. The actor standing right next to us.

Was this professionally appropriate? She held it up conspicuously when she handed it to me: she didn't care.

We met at her apartment, on East Sixth Street, tucked between restaurants on the famous old row of Bangladeshi restaurants. She was on Rollerblades. We drank bodega beer—Kingfisher—and walked on Second Avenue. Then she wanted to fuck me like I could not believe. She put me in a yellow chair, pushed me back, rode me, went down on me, rode me some more, went down on me some more, told me how she wanted me to come, and when, and where.

I got a migraine. I'd learned to heed a migraine's message, no matter how abrupt: go to a dark room, now.

I think the migraine had intervened.

My roommate, who had been up for a role in a movie the actor was producing, told me his calls weren't getting returned. Eventually, he got the story: "He doesn't want you in the movie because Doughty fucked his girlfriend."

He pointed out that *he* hadn't fucked anybody's girlfriend, but still didn't get the gig.

This actor got famous. Periodically, somebody who encountered him would tell me that he'd get maudlin and say, "Oh, you're friends with Doughty? He fucked my girlfriend."

Years later, I met him at a benefit we were both doing. I'd just gotten sober and had gained a bunch of weight. He thought I was one of those weirdos who thought I was a movie star's best friend.

I was wearing this black Paul Smith suit that I was extremely proud of—beautiful English-cut suit—and I joked, Looks like I'm the only one dressed for the gig. Like a joke on the thing where Wynton Marsalis used to get mad at jazz musicians for wearing T-shirts and fanny packs onstage.

The actor looked appalled.

But he felt bad when he discovered who the unrecognizable person was. He apologized, very kindly, then asked if I wanted to see a script he'd written.

Sure. You're a phenomenal artist, man; I'd love to do something.

He called, a day later, to say he wanted to clear the air. He went into an extensive explication of his feelings—went on forever—and said he could forgive me, but it was an awful thing for me to have done, and there was a level of trust that, etcetera.

I said something like, I can understand that?

I didn't say: I thought she was your assistant. I didn't fuck your girlfriend; your girlfriend fucked *me*.

PROFUSION (1990)

What happened to the Rollerbladers? They ruled New York.

You'd see chains of them hanging on to moving buses. When I was driving an ice-cream van, they'd shoot out from side streets, heedless of the lights, missing the van by seconds. I learned to check my blind spot three times before changing lanes.

I still do that: I'll be on an exit ramp in Oklahoma, checking for Rollerbladers.

NEARNESS (2015)

I got an email from Wayne Kramer saying he'd listened to the audiobook of my memoir. I chose to believe it was actually Wayne Kramer.

When I was a teenager, I read that the Sex Pistols liked the MC5's *Kick Out the Jams*, so I bought it. I was too young to understand it, but I wanted to understand it; I listened until I heard the beauty through the dissonance. I remember listening on a Walkman on a high-school field trip, looking around and realizing the other kids weren't capable of hearing beauty through the dissonance.

Wayne invited me to his studio the next time I was in Los Angeles; it was an office above a dry cleaner. I expected to find a sneering teenager, hysterical at my stupidity. But the man who answered the door was Wayne Kramer.

I asked him immediately if he wanted to start a band.

Brendan Canty from Fugazi flew in from DC to play drums. I hid when he got to Wayne's house; I'd seen Fugazi every time they played New York in the 1990s, and they intimidated the hell out of me.

I heard him laughing in the kitchen and came down to find not an austere, shirtless warrior, but a merry man with four kids in college.

We recorded at Henson, which has a statue of Kermit the Frog above its gate. Between takes, Brendan sat at a piano and played "The Nearness of You."

He told me that legends of Ethiopian jazz, now living in DC's huge Ethiopian community—the only American city to which there is a direct flight from Addis Ababa—gathered at his studio to play. He said it irritated them to discuss their records from the 1970s, from before the communist regime—phenomenal, African soul-jazz records.

When we mixed, I insisted that Wayne add some improvised guitar parts. He did. Every note, every sound, every string bend: genius. Brendan and I sat behind him, making ecstatic faces. It was a privilege, both hearing Wayne Kramer improvise, and experiencing euphoria in tandem with Brendan Canty.

The world was absolutely new.

After detonating space and time, Wayne turned around and said, "Anything else you want to do?"

NO FUTURE ONLY YOU (1994)

Wayne's solo debut and the first Soul Coughing album came out the same year; we both played the festival Les Trans Musicales, in Rennes. He said he saw us and suddenly believed that rock music was obsolete.

As I do about my music, now, when I hear new artists.

He said he could see that I was isolated, in a band that was contemptuous of me.

Soul Coughing never did as well in France as we did that night in Rennes. I remember the tremendous energy—I removed my shirt. Some French magazine printed a picture that I wish I could erase from my memory.

After the show, a French guy walked up and said, "There is no roots! There is no future! There is only you!"

COLLABORATORS (2016)

Wayne did over two years in prison in the 1970s; now he takes musicians to prisons to teach songwriting workshops, under the auspices of his charity Jail Guitar Doors—named after the Clash song, which *is about him.*

He took me to the LA Men's Central Jail—part of the LA County jail system—in downtown LA. Being there, he told me, meant you were on trial in a downtown LA courthouse or that you'd been convicted but had yet to be assigned to a prison—they called it *waiting to catch a chain.*

They took us to a room that smelled like busted pipes. Prisoners were sitting on folding chairs, in circles, some with guitars, some with cajóns. I went to a circle of guys shredding metal licks in their blue-and-yellow jumpsuits. They were shredding simultaneously—not together—with desperate relish; the instruments would soon be taken from them.

It was clear that each had a flawed command of social interaction. They'd run through their incredibly long song—the assigned topic: seven deadly sins—and abruptly one guy would stop to talk about how the song should break down for a riff he'd just come up with. Then a guy on a cajón would start practicing a rhythm that wasn't in the tune, and two guitar guys on the periphery would turn to each other and trade shreds.

Pretend you're on the Super Bowl! I said. A billion people are watching!

During the next run-through, one guy started talking; two guys yelped, "Super Bowl! Super Bowl!"

The cajón guy went into his own space again, as did a shred-trading duo and the guy who wrote lyrics, who also sat on a cajón; his right hand banged the two and the four, his left held a notebook.

How many verses have you written? I asked him gingerly.

"Seven," he said. "Because there's seven sins—?"

I suddenly understood that the important thing was to give these guys their moments. I said, I think every one of you guys should take a solo.

"Great idea! Great idea!!" they said.

The next problem was the order of soloists. In the middle of the first verse, one of them stopped abruptly to revise the batting order—"I think I should go first, and then it should be him, and . . ."

"Super Bowl!" yelled another guy.

We worked it out: I'd cue the soloist before a verse ended. We tried to run through it, but each guy panicked, fumbled the entrance, started talking over the song again, covering a fuckup with bluster.

They tried to put a guitar in my hands—because I did this for a living, I must be a samurai—but everything I know about lead guitar I'd learned from the solo on Neil Young's "Down by the River," which consists mostly of a single repeated note.

No, no, I said. This time is for you.

For the workshop assembly, the groups joined in a large circle, in a room that looked like a racquetball court. On the other side of a Plexiglas wall, medication call was happening: a nurse handed out paper cups of pills.

Behind another wall, prisoners loitered on a balcony and at tables welded to the floor. One guy on a bunk right up against the Plexiglas was reading a Ken Follett novel, which he held far above his face, touching the bunk above him, and then brought extremely close to his face. Unnervingly intimate to watch.

My guys were totally freaked out with stage fright.

The groups' songs were chaos, but each had one dude that was good. One guy was a great dancer, side-sliding on the shining floor;

there was an impressive singer, on par with, say, *American Idol* runners-up.

There was a guy named William whom I'd heard the other teachers talking about—they'd been trying to get him to collaborate. But tonight he played by himself, on cajón.

He began by asking a female guard to leave the room, telling her she'd be shocked by the song's content. She screwed up her mouth and shook her head. Unspoken: *I work in a jail.*

He beat out *bump-bump-bang*, pause, *bump-bang*, and sang a song called "Freaky Naughty Girl." The verses were sexy, but not enough to scare a prison guard.

The hook was: *Freaky naughty girl; freaky naughty. Freaky naughty girl; freaky naughty.*

It was spooky—magical—that he could make those particular words so mournful.

He wasn't quite in tune, which sounded exactly right.

Some guys put on stone faces to prevent emotional display.

As we drove away in Wayne's car, I bumped my fists softly against the dash—*bump-bump-bang*, pause, *bump-bang*—singing, *Freaky naughty girl; freaky naughty. Freaky naughty girl; freaky naughty.*

I woke up the next morning singing it: *Freaky naughty girl; freaky naughty. Freaky naughty girl; freaky naughty.*

VENDING

Wayne and I drove to the state prison at Norco, sixty miles from LA, with a trunk full of instruments for inmates. They wouldn't let us teach a workshop, but we could play a couple of tunes and Wayne would speak.

You're not supposed to wear jeans. I wore blue slacks—the wrong shade of blue. An aggro-avuncular guard told me, "You don't want those guys in the towers with the long-distance rifles to get you mixed up with an inmate."

We found a Target a few miles from the prison, and I bought the first pair of khakis I saw. I changed in the restroom.

Wayne, having been in prison, has something relevant to tell a convict; I don't. There were a couple of old white guys in the room—one asked whether the Amharic tattoo on my left arm was Celtic, which I took to mean *So, you're also a Nazi?*—but mostly it was younger black guys whom I thought would be disinterested in an acoustic version of "Super Bon Bon."

They were at the edges of their seats. They applauded fiercely. I don't think they knew the tune—and their reaction to the performance was, maybe, mostly about seeing any kind of performance whatsoever—but about a dozen guys shook my hand afterward and said, "Let the man go through!"

In the Q&A, somebody asked whether he was too old to get into the music business.

I said, Well, 2 Chainz is, like, fifty. They thought that was hilarious.

Their most probing questions were about an MP3 listening station in a common area at the prison. I didn't see it, and didn't quite understand the descriptions. They paid to hear songs on what sounded like a vending machine with cheap earphones attached—or it dispensed a preloaded MP3 player? They wanted to know how much of their money went to the musicians.

I tried to shrug off the question, saying I had no idea, but they persisted: Have you ever heard of anything like this? How much would you get paid for something similar to this? When they pay, is it treated more like a sale or a rental? Does the record company have to account to you for every single play? Do you get some kind of record of where and when it's been played?

Hesitantly I explained emerging-technologies clauses in record deals, how recoupment is a rigged game—the companies essentially have you agree to be in perpetual debt—and artists, even huge ones, are legally prevented from auditing them.

They seemed more fascinated by this than any other part of the Q&A.

Wayne and I sang "The Auld Triangle," a song about Mountjoy Prison in Dublin, where they banged a metal triangle to wake up the prisoners, to announce mealtimes, and to mark executions.

The old triangle goes jingle-jangle, all along the banks of the Royal Canal, goes the chorus.

I botched the harmony. It was great.

SENDING (1987)

I went to see the semester's-end recital for a class on Broadway musicals. My Parisian friend Jillian did "The Ladies Who Lunch." In fact, everyone did Sondheim.

A tiny girl sat at the piano and sang "Send in the Clowns." She had a fragile voice; there were pauses as her fingers carefully sought the chords. She stretched her toes to meet the pedals.

Everybody in the audience thought it was funny and great: How weird is it that this nerdy girl is in the Broadway class?

I sat in the back, weeping.

The world was absolutely new.

She loaned me twenty bucks once. I had to take the bus home to spend Thanksgiving in my family's sullen, periodically chaotic home. I was panicking in front of an ATM.

"What's wrong?" she asked. An open face: sincere concern.

I was dumbfounded when she offered to loan me twenty bucks; more so that she didn't seem suspicious. Who's nice? Nobody's nice. That was my world.

Before I returned to school, I asked my mom for twenty dollars to repay the girl. My mom got angry.

I immediately found the girl when I got back, gave her the money, and ran away. I was ashamed. She seemed to be taken aback that I'd considered it urgent to repay her. I never became her friend. I wish, I so wish, that I became her friend.

THREE INCHES
ABOVE THE FLOOR (1993)

Soul Coughing played CBGB during the New Music Seminar—bands at every venue in the city for four nights. We were on a bill with The The, Low, and five other bands.

We hadn't played CB's: they always put us in the 313 Gallery next door, where the quiet music went. We built a beautiful little scene around us there. Now I can see it was much more unique—and made much sweeter memories—than playing the main room could have. But at the time, the main room felt like an upgrade.

The dressing room was a plywood cubby behind the stage—no door. I found a note for The The taped to the wall, in a high school girl's bubble script: *Dear Matt Johnson, I came from Syosset to see you, could you please play the song 'This Is the Day'? I love you!!! Sincerely, Kristy heart heart heart*

We had yet to put out an album; this note would become familiar. If you were an artist on the margins, you had obsessive fans who were the one kid in their high school who'd heard of you.

For most bands, it was their catchiest song—they'd played it on Italian television and morning radio in Dallas and a hundred other times; for some bands, it was the song they were weary of playing, and if they allowed themselves cynicism, kids pleading for it felt like a violation.

Low had been produced by Kramer—the other Kramer—from the band Bongwater—a distinguished New York eccentric. He'd produced my favorite Galaxie 500 song, "When Will You Come Home." A warbly plaint soaked in echo.

I'd never heard them. I was leaning against the wall directly on the other side of the stage. The bass vibrated the wall and my body: single bass notes ringing forever.

It was so slow: marvelously slow.

I heard the vocal: *Three inches above the floor; man in a box wants to burn my soul.*

The world was absolutely new.

ADDENDUM ON
MARIO CALDATO JR. (2019)

I spent half the recording process for *Ghost of Vroom* concealing panic attacks. I'm really good at concealing them. I had extreme
impostor syndrome; constant nausea.

I'm a huge fan of the Beasties' ecosystem. The bands whose
overall aesthetic unity I've always wanted to emulate are the Dead,
Fugazi, and the Beasties.

When we were mixing, I read an interview with Adam Horovitz:
he said "Sabotage" was based on a joke about what a stress merchant
Mario was, pushing them to finish songs as if he wanted to fuck
them up.

Mario is the most dauntlessly mellow producer I've ever met.
Scrap and I had a joke imitation of him:

One of us: "Mario, how was that take?"

Imitation of Mario: (Beat. Beat. Beat. Beat. Beat. Beat. Beat.
Beat.) "Yeah!"

JEALOUS ECSTASIES (2013)

_____ had manic episodes; she'd accuse me of being attracted to people at random.

She freaked out about a Jennifer Lawrence poster in the Graham Avenue stop—which I don't think I'd looked at—stage-whispering, "Is that what you want?!"

Saying something shrinky like *I want you to know this is hurtful* made it worse. Countering with flattery made it much, much worse.

The manias were like epileptic fits—when exhausted, they were just gone. If I brought it up later, she had no idea what I was talking about.

CANDY (2014)

Until I was with _____, I thought ADHD was a hustle to get speed. But she needed her speed—though she didn't like it. I'm an addict in recovery, and I just couldn't bring myself to beg somebody, *Please take your speed, please just take your speed.*

She kept it in a drawer with the Advil. It said *amphetamine* right on the bottle. The day after Halloween one year, she went to CVS and bought fat bags of half-price candy. I asked her to hide them—for, in my heart, I am a fat man. But I never thought to ask her to hide the speed.

VERGE (1989)

I moved to New York on Easter. My dad drove me there in a beige Accord. With my Panasonic all-in-one stereo and a knockoff Fernandes Stratocaster in the trunk.

I rented a $350 room from a lady who owned a lot of books, on the Upper West Side: a realm of people who owned a lot of books. She wore beige turtlenecks and smoked Parliaments. She was the mother of a friend of mine from school. She needed dough, so she rented out her kid's room.

I ran out to the street to see my friends.

I saw a black woman striding across West Eighty-Eighth Street, in front of a store with a sign that said *HEBRAICA* (I had no idea what that was—lingual artifacts?). She wore a billowing shirt; a scarf at her throat. The world turned into grainy film and—in my mind's ear—piano-house music emanated from her.

I took the 1 train to Christopher Street and waited in front of a newsstand on Seventh Avenue, across from waves of people—most of whom I'm remembering to be white gay men, in their thirties, wearing turquoise Izod shirts—crossing Varick Street.

A shifty drunk paced between Village Cigars and Smiler's Never Closed. There was a laughing crowd outside Marie's Crisis.

My friends showed up and took me for falafel, which I'd never had before. Exotic! Cosmopolitan!

We went uptown to the Lincoln Square Cinemas and saw Pedro Almodóvar's *Women on the Verge of a Nervous Breakdown*. One of the stars was Rossy de Palma, a woman with an asymmetrical face—a melted-rhombus shape. Her eyes from two different faces. In the movie, she has moaning orgasms while sleeping in a lawn chair.

I went crazy for her in that dark theater. My New York dream was that I'd meet a girl like this: peculiar and orgasmic.

After the movie we smoked a pinner; we ran around singing Prince's "It's Gonna Be a Beautiful Night."

When I got back, my new landlady, or roommate, was awake, smoking and reading the *Village Voice*. I remember her ashtray resting on a *Voice* cover photo of Ron Vawter, a memory I can't trust because I would've had no idea who Ron Vawter was. She started complaining, and I felt trapped: I was higher than I thought I was.

I sat on the couch, trying to look normal.

She stopped herself.

"But you're young," she said in an exhausted tone, "and you probably see just the wonderful things in New York."

In my room, I turned on the Panasonic all-in-one and heard WBGO play John Coltrane's *A Love Supreme*—hearing it on a jazz station is slightly absurd, like actually hearing "Free Bird" on a classic-rock station. I'd never heard it before.

This is jazz? I thought. Jazz! *I am a guy who likes jazz!*

The fanfare at the top, that methodical, unforgettable bassline, the circular chanting.

The world was absolutely new.

On an island in the middle of Broadway, a homeless dude pushed a shopping cart; swollen bags of bottles were tied to the sides, as if for ballast; in the child-carry basket was a radio with a bent antenna, playing WBLS—Kool DJ Red Alert? That's my memory.

CRATE (1993)

I had a dairy crate of cassettes I'd been hauling around since the early 1980s. I was embarrassed by most of them.

I had a mixtape from the eighth grade titled *Wild Music*. On the flap I'd written descriptive copy in quotes, as if it had been blurbed: *This music is WILD!*

I was leaving CAT-BUKS and moving to Fort Greene—my first apartment without roommates. Three years later, Biggie's funeral would go past my front door.

I put the crate on the sidewalk, then ran upstairs to watch from five stories up whether someone would take some tapes.

Half my furniture I'd found abandoned on the sidewalk, including a massive orange fuzzy couch that I'd dragged by myself up the Bowery, passing a crowd in front of CBGB, who applauded me.

I only had to watch from the upstairs window for five minutes. Two black dudes walked by. One stopped. Pointed to the crate. They walked over hesitantly. One guy started sifting through them with one hand—his other in his jacket pocket. I figured this would be a bust—two black dudes, and the tapes were, like, the Cure and Ozzy. But they started grabbing cassettes, each cradling a dozen in their left arm, like infants. Then one of them had a visible epiphany. He picked up the box. The other hailed a cab.

They got in; they were gone.

It was like catching a perfect drama on surveillance footage.

I had a bunch of CDs, too, that I had accumulated in my job writing reviews for *NYPress*—stacks of completely random CDs I'd barely looked at. My roommates and I took them out of their cases and chucked them out the window like Frisbees. They smashed into splinters—spectacularly—on Fourteenth Street. We missed all the cabs, but somebody actually managed to land one in the bed of a pickup truck. To our loud hurrahs.

UNNECESSARY TOOLS (2015)

I got a text from a woman that _____ and I paid to clean our apartment when we moved out and I went to Memphis. _____ and I were pretending we weren't breaking up—that I was just moving eleven hundred miles away.

She worked at a hardware store near where _____ and I had lived; I'd had a crush on her, sometimes stopping in for unnecessary tools.

She texted—apropos of nothing—that she kept candy under her pillow to eat when she was half-asleep; she segued into talking about how nice her bed was; she segued into sending naked pictures.

I didn't want to be impolite, so I thanked her: I told her she was sexy.

She kept sending them.

I was stressed out. Shouldn't one do what one can to keep getting naked pictures? It was work! Constantly obliged to invent novel expressions of *Oh wow I'm so turned on.*

The less I texted back, the more pictures she sent.

Then she stopped.

She texted an apology a week later: she got a boyfriend.

Oh well, wasn't meant to be, I'm so sad, I told her.

PYRAMID (2016)

Months later, in a Facebook group for sober Brooklyn people, a friend posted a GIF of witches in a pyramid. It was meant to troll—affectionately—another friend: there was a group for sober women, and the joke we used to make was, *You're talking about me there, aren't you?? Aren't you??*

The thread went haywire—exploding with recriminations.

My friend was mortified and apologized in detail. He did the thing where you stop using contractions, to show how contrite you are.

Then he deleted the thread. Now people were enraged: he'd erased them!

The woman from the hardware store—also in the sober Facebook group—rained hellfire in the comments.

I did something foolish: I defended him. There are awful people in this world, malicious people—but not this guy.

I felt like the deposed emperor in *The Last Emperor*: now an obscure citizen working in a Beijing flower shop, he steps up to defend his good-hearted former jailer, whom the Red Guards are parading in chains and a dunce hat.

She sent me a blazing, novella-length DM.

I scraped and bowed, really—expressing both my actual politics and my fear of ostracism. Then, my phone buzzed: a Venmo request—I didn't even remember signing up for Venmo?—for $65.

It said, *For emotional labor.*

FOLDING (1989)

The day after we saw *Women on the Verge of a Nervous Breakdown*, I went looking for a job. First, to Canal Jean: they weren't looking for anybody, but I saw Downtown Julie Brown among the racks.

I went to a store in a dilapidated building farther south, called Alice Underground, a vast secondhand-clothes store of a disappearing type: genuinely cheap clothes.

I spoke to an old lady with a Ukrainian accent. She was folding ratty shirts with delicate movements.

"How old are you?" she asked, her eyes on the shirts.

I told her I was eighteen.

"You are so young," she said.

I was offended. Young? I was eighteen!

I was trying to look tough.

"I pay you five dollars an hour," she said. "Come tomorrow."

She didn't tell me what time tomorrow; she didn't hand me an application or get a Social Security number from me. Five dollars an hour was not enough to live on, even with my exceptionally cheap rent.

I didn't come back on Monday.

From every unchosen choice at that age, I see strange and magical paths. My guess in retrospect is that Alice Underground paid employees off the books—maybe I could've gotten by without taxes taken out? The place was staffed with sullen art teens of the kind I longed to befriend in New York. Who would I have met? What would've happened?

Two friends of mine worked at a store on West Broadway—just when upscale boutiques were appearing there. It sold linen clothes that looked good on divorced white women. They steered me into a job, pretending to the manager that they didn't know me, as they'd previously had to pretend not to know each other.

They were black, and both of them—like every black person I was friends with—had insisted to me, at some point, that when they went to stores they were followed around by security. I could never believe it.

The manager told me, as she hired me, to keep an eye on black kids and not let them go into the changing booth.

I ate lunch on West Broadway, on a metal stoop. A guy who looked like H. R. Haldeman in a lumberjack costume sat down next to me; he told me I reminded him of his dead son. I gave him my condolences. He said that the song "My Way" had been stolen from his mind, and that they should buy Atlantic City and give it to the homeless.

I commuted there on the subway every day from the Upper West Side. It unnerved and fascinated me that New Yorkers were so mesmerized by their interiors. I switched trains via the pedestrian tunnel on Fourteenth Street. I loved the sound of the footsteps and yelps echoing down the tile.

I got fired after a woman, while trying on pleated khakis, asked me if she looked slutty. I replied, indignantly, that I had no idea.

GRAND (1996)

I stayed at the SoHo Grand in 1996, just after it'd been built.

I didn't live anywhere, because I was always on tour, and Warner Bros. liked Soul Coughing enough to pay for whatever could be tenuously connected to promotion. When I wasn't on tour I crashed with a girlfriend in London or a tour manager's friend in Pensacola. Warner Bros. would pay for hotels and business-class flights, but I didn't make enough money to have an apartment.

The SoHo Grand was across the street from where that boutique had been. I had a room ten stories above West Broadway; I looked down on it and tried to feel like I'd won. Instead I felt shame for having been fired in 1989. That's my brain.

ADDENDUM ON
CANAL JEAN (1984, 2009)

In my high school—James I. O'Neill High School—if you wore a Canal Jean pin, it meant you bought clothes in Manhattan. It was like alternate-reality school spirit.

I don't know why James I. O'Neill chose as school colors that gruesome gold and maroon.

I went on the internet looking for a Canal Jean pin to wear in a suit lapel, like a senator wears a tiny flag. I was shocked to find that Canal Jean still existed—in an outer-borough warehouse, behind a Petco.

On Google Street View, I swear I could see through the glass to the racks: knockoff FUBU and JNCO.

IDENTITIES (2017)

I stalked _____'s Instagram profile as a mood stimulant. I couldn't look at her stories, though, without her being able to see that I was looking. So I started a pseudonymous account: @OfficialCarlosGardel.

Carlos Gardel was a tango singer who died in a plane crash in 1935. It's the only name I came up with that wasn't taken.

I screen-shot pics of Carlos Gardel from other accounts. I found murals of him in Montevideo; I found a meme of Drake being sad about a Uruguayan flag that said Gardel, and happy about an Argentine flag that said Gardel—there's a dispute over which country can claim him. I found steak houses named after him in Melbourne and Bangkok.

I wrote a mini-bio with Google Translate but realized that the text would read as fake to a Spanish speaker.

I decided instead to be Danish: I concocted a bio meant to seem unsophisticated—I used shooting-star and blue-heart emojis—and started using *lånt fra*, "borrowed from," when reposting. I don't think Danes say that on Instagram—I made it up.

My phone's autocorrect actually learned the phrase.

I tagged tango fans so they'd follow back, which would make it look less fake. They left encouraging comments, clearly using Google to translate Spanish to Danish. *This random, cute Danish fan!*

I told friends, who all followed the account—but I panicked and blocked them. I guess I could've asked nicely for them to unfollow, but it would've taken longer. What if she looked at @OfficialCarlos Gardel's follower list and saw people she knew were my friends?

SALE (2001)

I went to Shanghai a month after 9/11. The ticket was cheap; I found a luxe hotel at airport-motel prices.

I got my visa at the Chinese consulate in New York, which is in a former Howard Johnson's hotel on Twelfth Avenue. Not to say it's a bizarre contrast: the Howard Johnson's must've looked more like a tower of authoritarian bureaucracy than the Chinese consulate looks like a 1970s tourist hotel.

Falun Gong protestors across the street were staging tableaux of communists committing acts of torture. Not scenes, but tableaux: they posed, holding batons aloft over a chained man.

PASS

When I connected in San Francisco, I had my passport checked three times.

At my gate, a cop was questioning a scared teenager. A Saudi Arabian passport was on the counter in front of him. He was dressed in what he must've thought would appear to be respectable business attire, but looked more like the clothes a seventh grader would throw together to play Willy Loman: cheap brown sport coat, boat shoes with black athletic socks, wrinkled blue suit pants, a silk tie, a yellow Ralph Lauren shirt that had been washed a hundred times; the collar had rolled.

SURCHARGE

I was nearly alone in the immense Shanghai airport. I got the lone taxi. The ride was endless—endless—on a deserted highway of immaculate asphalt, to 金茂大廈: the Golden Prosperity Building.

At last the tiny Honda pulled up to a massive, latticed-steel tower.

I'd changed dollars to yuan, but was iffy on the rate: I squinted at the meter, certain I was misreading. That's, like, twenty bucks? No. Can it be two hundred? More likely than twenty, right? For a ride that long?

I stuck a deck of yuan notes through the partition. The driver looked at it, puzzled. Then his eyes popped. He snatched it.

I knew I'd fucked up.

I found myself on the curb with my bag.

"Yes thank you okay thank you goodnight goodnight," he said. He scrambled to get the cab in gear and screeched away.

The hotel lobby, on a high floor of the Golden Prosperity Building, was a brass cathedral, with abundant beige couches as deep as beds. Tall windows with spectacular views across the river to the Bund. A roar of colors glowed behind the skyline. Beams of blue light whipped across the clouds.

I was checked in by a Chinese guy with a Cockney accent as sharply drawn as his courtesy.

I spent hours obsessed with my stupidity. Two hundred bucks! Retracing the moment I put the money in the slot; angry at the cab driver, angry at myself.

Here I was in this lavish room. I once bought a jacket for two hundred bucks and never wore it—it looked different in daylight—and shrugged it off. But how often does a Shanghai cab driver get an unexpected $200? What a day he had.

KIOSKS SOLD
TRANSLUCENT WINGS

南京路, a long shopping street, is Shanghai's Times Square or Shibuya—maybe more Times Square than Times Square, more Shibuya than Shibuya. At night, it looks like they put up extra moons.

By the enormous KFC—three stories of KFC exploding with digital crawls, the Colonel's face whirling, expanding, splitting—a girl waved me down. She wore pink inflatable angel wings. She was with a pack of girls in identical shirts, some also wearing inflatable wings—reflected Colonels spinning in the translucent plastic.

They surrounded me.

Another girl buttonholed a passerby and handed him a camera. I was the center of a group photograph. They shook my hand, one by one, giddily.

I passed another bewildered white dude surrounded by schoolkids. So this is standard in the school-trip experience: *Get pics with Whitey!*

The wings were the must-have teen-tourist accessory, sold from carts and kiosks everywhere. The street crawled with laughing teenagers in translucent pink angel wings.

LUTE

Outside a 7-Eleven, a crazy lady—I could tell by her busted red umbrella and the copious space pedestrians gave her—walked up and yelled, "大鼻子!"

Long nose: an old-fashioned epithet.

I waited out the rain in a music store on a side street. I bought a tenor lute: a 中阮. The crusty guy running the shop wrote *40* on a piece of paper—forty yuan for the lute—I nodded.

I wanted extra strings: ten sets, because when would I come back to Shanghai? There's a Chinese system of hand signals I saw in a guidebook: I did the signal for ten—a cross with your index fingers. Proud of myself for the insider move.

He scoffed explosively. Someone I took for a daughter or niece—because an employee wouldn't yell at her boss—snapped at him like, *Don't be a dumbass, he wants extra strings.*

He opened a drawer and took out ten packs. Grunting neutrally.

It's great to carry an instrument because people think you're going somewhere. I walked purposelessly up and down the 南京路.

I sat on a bench shaped like an open ledger. A man in a white polo shirt sat down next to me.

He spoke to me like he was trying to reason with a drunk. I referred to a part of Shanghai by one of its historical names: the French Concession. He insisted no such place ever existed.

I finally introduced myself and stuck out my hand. He shook it with weary annoyance and left.

I carried the lute to a promenade overlooking the river. In 1993, the Chinese government decided it was necessary to have a skyline;

the skyscrapers look like they were drawn on a coaster: "There'll be one that looks like a flower, and one that looks like a robot linebacker, and one with a hole in it, and, like, the Eiffel Tower with pink spheres!"

A green screen was set up on the promenade: guys in referee shirts were selling digital portraits. They superimposed your choice of background; most of the available backgrounds were the tallest spire in the skyline: 東方明珠塔, the Oriental Pearl Radio and Television Tower—the Eiffel Tower with pink spheres.

If you had a camera and just turned around, you could have your picture taken in front of the *actual* 東方明珠塔.

I got a green-screen pic. I would've made it an album cover if I weren't so fat.

The guys in the referee shirts wanted to see my *Lonely Planet*; they turned to the dictionary in the back, pointing at the entries, laughing. It was ordered in the Roman alphabet, so in Mandarin it was a random list.

DUOS

I kept being approached by duos of young people who told me—furtively?—that they were students from Xi'an participating in an art show. Did I want to see it?

They were strangely deferential.

I never learned what the art show was, or what was going down—were they trying to rob me? Pitch a religion? Ask me to smuggle something?

They'd shake my hand, resigned, and leave.

AURA

I was staring at the Shanghai Museum, built to resemble a gigantic cooking pot, when I saw the aura that precedes a migraine. A migraine sends a message: *Go to a dark room.*

I took a cab back to the Golden Prosperity Building.

I met a cheerful old Chinese couple in the elevator; they asked me if I was carrying a guitar. I told them it was a 中阮.

Do you play it?

No, I play guitar.

They laughed.

The elevator stopped; they gestured for me to exit. I said, No, no, you first, and they told me I should go first, and then I said they should, and we did this four times, until at last they walked out, pleased.

I correctly performed the politeness dance!

I slept off the migraine and woke at midnight. From the hotel bed I looked out over the river at the shifting lights on the row of Baroque Revival banks; foreign powers had built them before the First World War, when Shanghai was an interzone.

This was October 7, 2001. Less than a month before, the Golden Prosperity Building had been the fifth tallest in the world. Now it was the fourth.

I turned on the TV; I plucked the lute. On CNN, the bombing of Kabul began.

JEEP BEATS (1989)

My memory is that lower Broadway was bumper-to-bumper Geo Trackers—nothing but Geo Trackers—with huge bass systems, competing bass drops reverberating between buildings. Giant low notes shifting as the car passed: the Doppler effect.

Geo Trackers weren't Jeeps, but the music was called *jeep beats*.

In my mind, all the Geo Trackers were a particular green. The particular frequency of a jeep beat's bass note—a trace of buzzing vehicle-body—still sounds to me like a deep forest green.

I was standing in the liminal space between the McDonald's and Shakespeare and Company, watching girls pass in and out of the Tisch building. Girls who went to the acting school at NYU. White Adidas on my feet and a dime bag in my pocket—which I'd just bought at Record-A-Rama—a front, with sun-faded record sleeves stapled to the walls—on Avenue A.

I heard De La Soul's "The Magic Number" coming from a Geo Tracker stopped at a light.

The world was absolutely new.

I nearly ran to Tower Records. I couldn't find the tape. I scanned the same racks repeatedly, pacing up and then back down the aisle, thinking I failed to see it. Crazy-person thinking.

A girl was stacking boxes. She told me they were out: people had been coming into Tower for days wanting De La Soul.

I was never able to be charming. As a teenager, I was slender, had long blond hair, and my Elizabethan paleness seemed lit from the inside. But I carried myself as I saw myself: a boy who was angry about being unattractive.

I mustered every resource to be charming. Made eye contact. Are you *sure* there aren't any in the back?

She smiled shyly. She told me she had hidden one cassette, for herself. She told me to follow her. We went to the classical section, where she had cached the tape in a little-perused rack. She handed it to me.

PIG, ELF (1990)

We all went to a Canadian friend's apartment, on East First Street, and took LSD she'd bought in Guelph. The hits had pictures of Porky Pig.

Her brother showed us lighting tricks he was learning in film school. We listened to "Yummy Yummy Yummy" by the Ohio Express and "1, 2, 3 Red Light" by the 1910 Fruitgum Company—terrifying songs if you're on acid.

A friend of theirs had some hilarious answering-machine message, which everybody but me had heard by now. I was handed the phone.

I heard a sped-up *yeedle-deedle* voice rhyming about elves in top hats.

Then it went *glgk!* and there was a different voice, slurred and weepy. "Hello—hello?—hello?—I knew it would be you—I knew you'd call me."

My Canadian friend was looking at me like, *So funny, right? Right?*

The slurred voice in my ear: "I can hear you!—Why are you doing this to me? *Why* are you doing this to me? Why are you *doing* this to me?"

The receiver felt like putty fusing to my head.

Now wailing. "I know you're there I know you're there I know you're there—I know you're there!—talk to me—talk to me!" I don't know how much time passed. Acid hours.

"Is it still going?"

She took the phone. The guy in Guelph had been crawling on his floor, puking on himself. He thought I was his girlfriend.

91

SNOW, EPISODE (1992)

I had to work during a blizzard.

The Knitting Factory's new manager was named David Brenner—like the comedian—and was hired because he'd actually manage the place. He didn't get high in the office; we had to do our jobs.

I sat at the towering desk, smoking, smoking, smoking. The downstairs bar was deserted except for me and the goth-y, yoga-teaching bartender—she leaned against the register, arms folded, glaring at nothing.

Meticulous bebop floated downstairs from the performance space: Paul Motian's electric band. Seven people paid to see the early set.

Nobody paid for the late set. David Brenner let me leave at midnight.

I walked up Broadway in the snow. Taxis plowed through the fluff. The snowflakes billowed in lights.

I had an Etta James tape—I'm not sure where I procured it—on the Walkman.

The beatific strings, and her voice: the color of brass, the texture of skin.

My pace synced to the orchestra—an elegant trudge.

On the last word of the line *We're drinking my friend to the end of a brief episode*, her voice dropped—second syllable—perilously falling—flying back up—buttoning the word without changing stride.

It's like when you accidentally touch a hot stove, and there is a long moment outside of time where you're thinking, *I have touched a hot stove. I regret touching this hot stove. This hot stove will cause imminent pain. I am about to be in pain from touching the hot stove. Here I am, waiting to experience pain from touching the hot stove.*

Then, you're back, and yelping.

Time slows down, like that, for the last syllable of the word *episode.*

Teenagers were running in the snow on Houston Street, skidding and howling.

The world was absolutely new.

I AM THE ONE CANADIAN (1996)

There was something very 1970s about the Guelph siblings—and in fact about a whole network of Guelph kids who came to New York. The whole coterie had an affinity for kitsch: the aesthetic of wide collars, sitcom laughs, macramé, disco strings, Lite-Brite, Lee Majors, striped Chevelles, Rufus Xavier Sarsaparilla.

I smuggled some mushrooms into Canada. At customs, I was wearing this XXXL maroon school jacket I'd found. A football team called the Rockets.

"Hello, Doc," said a cop. "Doc. Doc! Earth to Doc!"

He was talking to me. I had never noticed—in the months I'd worn the Rockets jacket—that *Doc* was stitched on it in white thread.

"Get those ears checked, Doc," he said.

I ate the mushrooms—they tasted like particleboard—at the hotel in Toronto.

I lay down on the bed and closed my eyes.

I had a vision of the 1970s—in my consciousness, the spirit of Canada had become the spirit of Guelph-kitsch. I heard something like the theme from *The Rockford Files* and saw rushing past my face—on a rainbow of avocado green, autumn brown, harvest gold, burnt orange—station wagons, Jill Whelan, the Honeycomb Kids, the Bay City Rollers.

How was it so sinister?

The trip wisped away quickly. I turned on CNN.

My British girlfriend called. I had given her the list of numbers for all the hotels I'd be in for six weeks. She was in a ruinous depression. What's happening?

"A plane from Nairobi crashed into the sea," I said. "They found the *four Americans* and the *five Swedes*, but they haven't found *the one Canadian*."

"I am that one Canadian!" she yelled.

961

I found out years later that I knew someone on that flight: Ethiopian Airlines Flight 961, on the twenty-third of November, 1996, taken by hijackers who demanded to be flown to Australia. She had begun to hate her job, so she quit to spend a year traveling with a friend. It was the second day of her year off. She survived.

HE SURE COULD
FLY THAT PLANE (1987)

I quit a job at McDonald's. They had me working the pie fryer: lower the basket into the oil, hit the buzzer, wait, pull up the basket, hit the buzzer.

I asked if I could pull a chair over. The manager was discomfited.

There was an industrially-produced buzzer used in the machine: I hear it sometimes in alarm clocks and other things. I was sixteen, and I'm in my fifties as I write this: the sound still sends me—for a bottomless moment—to where nothing is good in the world and I'm trapped in it.

When I said I was leaving, another kid working a fryer yelled indignantly, "Two weeks' notice! Two weeks' notice!"

I had gotten another job, at the cadet laundry during field training. It paid $6.25 an hour, which was shocking money. McDonald's, like most jobs, paid minimum wage: $3.35.

Bags of BDUs—battle dress uniforms—came off trucks, were dumped on tables, we stapled tags on them—*chdk! chdk! chdk!*—and threw them down a chute.

We had to be there at five.

There were two women always talking in Tagalog: *something something something something fucking BDUs!*

We worked in teams—tag-tearer and staple-wielder—and I was put with a glum woman who seemed to hate me. Would only grunt when I said good morning.

One day, out of nowhere, she said, "Did you see _____ last night?" naming a movie on TV.

She was smiling. I said yes.

"He sure could fly that plane!" she said.

97

CRAWL (2008)

I was in Spain with my girlfriend; she was doing a show there. I watched a performance—genius show—and told her I'd like to spend the next night drinking coffee on the plaza.

She reacted as if cruelly betrayed.

So I watched every performance—four nights and a matinée. I sat next to her during the show as she loudly scribbled notes for the actors. Nonstop. In the dark hall, no sound but the manic scribbling.

The next night, passive-aggressively, I criticized the ending. She kept me up all night, eviscerating me. I scraped, I pleaded: no use. The blue light pooled under the curtains, then dawn, then morning.

One of my saddest experiences: walking into a Spanish café at 4:30 p.m. and asking, ¿Desayunos?

I journaled in the peach-colored lobby, waiting for a car. *Why do I stay if she's cruel and controlling? What about _____, who I really want to be with?*

The upholstery was nearly threadbare. There was a stand of sun-faded tourist pamphlets by the check-in desk, which had been pocked by years of suitcases banging it at handle level.

An elderly man in a dusty-tan suit—an *elderly* elderly man— wore a ratty toupee, asymmetrically: the hairstyle of heartthrobs circa 1978. Even if the toupee didn't look like it'd been fished from a trash can, it would be bizarrely discontinuous with his head.

He sank in the sofa as if under the toupee's weight. His hands rested on a cane. He glared indignantly into space—like a deposed-baron glare.

I put my camera on the journal and clicked the button while looking in another direction. A fabulous composition: the toupéed man in sharp focus above the blurred text, which looked like the expository crawl before *Star Wars*.

I blogged the photo at the airport, where there was wi-fi.

My girlfriend effortlessly read the journaling. She was a Shakespearean scholar, and had been taught to read smudged manuscripts and, like, Elizabethan shopping lists.

When I landed, my phone went *blrrlp!* and there was an unglued voicemail from her.

I'd been writing a song called "I Keep on Rising Up," as an exercise; my music-publishing rep had sent me a list that was surreptitiously circulating around her company: themes that advertising agencies asked for:

Fun love
Sun/sunshine
Succeeding
Winning
Rising
The good old days
Female empowerment
Coming home
Togetherness

Why secret? Why not send it to writers?

She told me it was offensive. Like line-readings for actors.

I wrote for every theme but female empowerment. I did a thing that I love in songs: agonizing verses, soaring chorus. Like how "Every Breath You Take" is about a stalker, and "California Dreamin'" is about winter despair.

"I Keep on Rising Up" contains the line *You're like trying to sleep off a cocaine binge.*

INSIDE

We thought about writing something together. She floated a title. I said I was hoping for a cooler one—that's the word I used.

She turned on me with giant eyes of fury.

"So, what, then—'*Cool Joe Hill, the Skateboarding Dog*'???"

We laughed—the argument broke as a fever breaks.

I live for inside jokes. I pick up friends' inside jokes, even without context: I love the rhythm of an inside joke.

People stay in relationships for sex; for affection; for money. I stayed for Cool Joe Hill the skateboarding dog.

TAPPING

We took a literal holiday in Cambodia—which is what you should do as your relationship dies its sour death. In Kampot, we stayed at a charming hotel in which we had the very worst room: a windowless box.

I took my laptop to a picnic table on the roof: a view of a disused bridge, and a breeze over a green river. You could smell the jungle scraping corrugated-iron roofs.

Wi-fi was still miraculous. I was arranging a show in Ohio with an agent in Marin County and a manager in London.

Someone on Facebook posted an old interview with the skater Andy Kessler—a friend. Someone posted a skate video. Somebody posted an old picture.

Why is everyone posting about Andy? Oh.

I knew he was dead.

He'd been stung by a bee while surfing and died of an allergic reaction.

I let out a groan of shock. A merry Australian guy was at the bar. "Well, that doesn't sound like good news!"

A friend of mine died, I said.

"Well. I didn't mean. I'm sorry. I was. I didn't." He was mortally embarrassed.

I spent a long time making sure this stranger didn't feel bad for inadvertent glibness. That's my brain.

I went back to our room. She was tapping fiercely on her laptop. She had a practice of automatic writing, typing without intention for hours and hours; her unconscious emerged from under her hands.

A friend of mine died, I said.

She stopped tapping, looked up at me with no expression.

BILL THE WIZARD (2010)

I went to twelve-step meetings in the East Village with a guy we called Bill the Wizard. A nebbishy, compassionate guy. He'd been in prison in Florida. He had fascinating, sad tales of his fellow convicts—baffled, crushed human beings. He pointed out that some people we knew who'd spent time in prison still ate with elbows in front of their plates, guarding their food.

We both lived on the Lower East Side during 9/11. We talked about how violating it felt when truther kids played dorm-room spooky-spy.

Like JFK stuff, right?

"Oh, but *that* was a setup," said Bill.

A MAN STANDS
NEXT TO A LIGHT (2000)

I saw a Xerox taped to a pole on Rivington Street: an O-Town video would be shot there. It said, *Thank you for the tremendous color and energy of your neighborhood.* Signed, publicist for a production company.

This was for *an O-Town video.*

Productions were constantly in my neighborhood: kid gofers would jump from nowhere, asking me to stand and wait.

I said: I live here, I don't care, I don't care, I live here, I don't care.

I bumped past a frantic gofer one night and walked into a bodega, where an irritated man stood by a big light.

"Yeah, go ahead, buy anything you want," he sneered.

I thought: I'm going to channel-surf past whatever movie this is at two in the morning and think, I'm glad I had that Fruitopia.

When I left the bodega, I saw Robert De Niro, sitting in a vintage Oldsmobile and glaring at me for fucking up his take.

JUST ONE DAY
OUT OF LIFE (1985)

Nobody remembers how they interrupted Live Aid every fifteen minutes for Sally Field. The same promo, unchanging, all day, unrelentingly: doe eyes, corny script. They cut from bands— mid-performance!—to Sally Field, apropos of nothing.

I was vigilant. Led Zeppelin was coming. When will Led Zeppelin come? What if they cut from Led Zeppelin to Sally Field?

They didn't broadcast Led Zeppelin. The most I would see was an aside from Dick Clark while he interviewed some mook. "And you can hear Led Zeppelin onstage behind us."

Madonna's set was in the late afternoon: not a prestige slot. Before the stars-and-stripes curtain opened on her band, she was shown grimly conferring with a stage manager with a towel around his neck. She pointed to her mic, to the monitors, while he nodded.

Bette Midler introduced her. The audience—hours drunk in the sun—chanted what sounded like *Styx! Styx! Styx!* but Styx wasn't playing.

My tastes were: boy, suburbs, white. Who's interested in Madonna? Was anybody?

Madonna wore an oversized blazer in July. Her two dancers had gold crosses hanging from their ears.

She was a star.

She opened with "Holiday," a strangely sad song. Pleading: *Just one day out of life.*

I didn't know how I felt about this performance as I watched it. To enjoy it would've been contrary to my principles.

A squelching dance-music bass played the melancholy progression.

What's so melancholy about that progression? I looked up the chords online, parsed them on guitar. It's uncanny.

I knew that AIDS was happening in the city: everybody was dancing, now everybody's dying. It was the age of the word *party*, but the song doesn't contain it. The refrain not beseeching but wistful: *It would be so nice.*

The world was absolutely new.

ADDENDUM ON PRINCIPLES

Though I adjured her not to, my mom filled out a card to win tickets to the Jacksons' *Victory* tour. We were at the Burger King near the Nanuet Mall. I was having a veal parmigiana.

I was so angry. Did she think I'd go with her?

ADDENDUM ON MADONNA'S DAUNTLESS HUSTLE

I don't know if AIDS was—explicitly or implicitly—the subject of "Holiday," and I don't know if that uncanny progression was intended to sound sad. It seems more likely she was going for a dance-floor perennial, like Kool and the Gang's "Celebration."

Have you ever counted the hooks on "Celebration"? Put it on. An absurd number of iconic hooks. There's four before they get to the first verse.

PROJECTIONS (2012)

A woman on Tinder had written her profile in half-disguised twelve-step argot. *Attitude of gratitude,* etc. I asked her out.

I searched her full name, and found—wedged among her corporate headshots—a picture of her in a bikini, in a bathroom stall, with a tiny gold marijuana leaf dangling from a belly-button piercing.

We went to the Rubin Museum, which exhibits Asian artifacts. I had done a show there once as part of a themed series: artists explored the galleries with a guide, stopping in front of a piece that attracted them. The guide would explain it. You'd have slides of these pieces projected behind you; between songs, you'd talk about what attracted you to them.

All the pieces I liked were images of Vajrabhairava, a death god who kills death itself. All different: in sexual congress with his consort (a living corpse); surrounded by shining waves; yowling with a ferocious mouth.

I didn't do it on purpose. I ambled toward things I liked and the guide would say, "This, again, is Vajrabhairava, a god of death . . ."

Being in recovery is great for date conversation: *To me, the seventh step is severely underrated.* Then she talked about her job: she was an accountant at Fox News. Just an accountant, she stressed! Actually it's a great place to work!

"I'll tell people I was a crackhead before I tell them I work at Fox," she said.

KNOT ROOM (1992)

The Knot Room was a brick storage space at the Knitting Factory, converted into a lo-fi venue. If you were somebody who sent in a demo tape and just wouldn't stop calling, they booked you in the Knot Room.

There was a five-dollar Monday night performance-art showcase called House of Ill Repute—they had a policy of canceling any show at which the audience could conceivably win a fight with the performers.

When it was empty, a barback, _____, hung out in there and shot dope. He was a mopey Brazilian guy—one of those ageless dope fiends that could've been thirty or sixty. He had a slack, sad face.

He would come up to us when the club was jammed—we were madly restocking beer—and ask in a gentle voice, "Please may I have some red wine?" Holding out his glass.

We'd yell at him, snatching the glass, and throw a bin in his arms, pointing angrily to the bottles accumulating on the floor.

Everybody secretly loved him.

One of the bartenders put on a play in the Knot Room and cast him as a sleeping man. The cast of characters in the program said:

Sleeping Man . . . . . . _____

It was a two-hour show, and I think _____ was really sleeping.

I recorded songs during the day with the house engineer, using the club as a makeshift studio (eventually that's how I recorded

110

the Soul Coughing song "Janine"). I had _____ read an absurdist poem while a cello player and I noodled avant-gardily.

The last line of the poem—declaimed sleepily by _____—was, "The FBI does not want the people to get together and love one another."

APPARITIONS

There were people we called apparitions: Were they being deliberately wonderful or being themselves without effort?

I wanted to be one. But it's no light commitment, being an apparition.

There was a guy who wore tree branches, stomping around St. Mark's Place (he's thanked in the liner notes of Jeff Buckley's *Live at Sin-é* as Tree Man); a woman who had shaved off her eyebrows and painted blue rectangles in their place; a man with a camera made of plastic bottles who acted like he was taking your picture, signaling for you to turn your face and pose.

There was an elderly guy with hair like a black plastic hat; he wore a checkered sport coat and heavy makeup—red circles on his cheeks. He yelled out, "Gene Krupa! Chick Webb! Louie Bellson!" while imitating their styles, flailing drumsticks on garbage cans, or on invisible drums in empty air.

There was a man called the Duck Man who appeared as if from nowhere, like *Brigadoon*, with a towering cart of identical stuffed animals. He was in the movie *Basquiat*: Jeffrey Wright sees him randomly and runs after him, yelling, "Duck Man!! Duck Man!!"

_____was an apparition. I never got much of his story, but I heard something about a wife and kids in São Paulo. I imagine him coming to New York on a vacation or to study, sniffing a bag of dope with another tourist in the bathroom at Phebe's and realizing he'd found his life. Plenty of people came to New York, from around the world, to be dope fiends. It was one of the New York dreams.

PRESS

I took a wild shot at a job reviewing music for *NYPress*; they'd ran a classified. I sent them a letter: all lies. I invented a quote from Antonin Artaud.

I got a message from John Strausbaugh, the editor, which was stunning: I read *NYPress* every week, and loved his stories about UFOs, immortal cranks, Elvis worship. Strausbaugh should be recognized as an essential voice of New York counterculture in the '90s and an important figure in the history of New York journalism.

I'm certain that John could spot a hustle, and that's why he gave me the gig.

I had no idea what the work entailed. I just started walking into places, writing about whatever music happened to be there. One night I wandered into a place and watched a girl—maybe a waitress there?—sing Broadway tunes. Innocent and corny.

She reminded me of NYU acting school kids who wore sweat-shirts from their summer drama camps; if they had a party and you looked at their CDs, you always saw Billy Joel's *Greatest Hits*—both volumes—and *The Original London Cast Les Misérables the Musical Sensation*.

I wrote a shitty review. Maybe eight hundred words, which is what you needed to get paid $75 by *NYPress*. It was mean. It was detailed. It was resentment of those drama school kids, who I thought didn't like me. It was my thing: feeling threatened by happy people, responding with dismissive cruelty.

I can't imagine what it was like to open up a newspaper and find a cruel dissection by some kid who'd gotten his job with faked Artaud quotes.

There was a letter in the issue after the review ran, from a co-worker of the singer: *At least she's getting up there and creating something!*

It would be easy to say I didn't care about the letter—that's what any critic would say—but it froze my blood.

I wish I could tell her how sorry I am. It was unconscionable. Bad reviews make you feel assaulted; you become paranoically ashamed, as if everybody on the subway is thinking mocking thoughts. I remember the first bad review I ever got—it was full-body hurtful.

I've gotten many, many hurtful reviews.

I did it for $75. I did it because I thought *she* thought she was better than me: I was just being as grandiose as I was paranoid, because why would she think of me at all?

There's a thing in the twelve-step universe called the amends; it's distinct from an apology. Addicts leave trails of apologies, *sorry sorry sorry sorry sorry sorry sorry*; a real amends is a sincere expression of regret, not to smooth things over but to get weight off your heart.

Were I her, I don't know that I'd accept an apology.

With all of my heart—not just with my heart, but with my lungs and my nervous system—I apologize to you, whoever and wherever you are. I would do anything to not have done it. Sometimes I regret it so much I put my head in my hands and wish to stop existing.

VACANT PLATE (1999)

A dude I knew invited me to Albert Maysles's place. How did he know Albert Maysles? But there we were, in the Dakota, in Albert Maysles's majestic dining room.

He sat at the table's head: swoop of white hair, tortoiseshell glasses; very skinny old man. Slight Dorchester accent.

These were my heroin days. They brought out food, but I didn't eat and didn't want to pretend. I sat with a clean white plate in front of me.

I went into the bathroom—a chamber of royal marble—tapped a line of dope on the sink, and sniffed it. I came back, sat in front of my vacant plate, and nodded out.

I don't remember bringing it up, but I'd been making rinky-tink dance music at home, on a Roland Groovebox. I could never remember what I'd done, so I used to turn on a camcorder, point it at a wall, and let the audio capture the music. I still have a stack of DV tapes marked *Groovebox*. I've never listened.

Somebody said Albert was making a film where they needed some '80s-sounding music. Was it him, or a producer, or someone random at the dinner?

I said, Oh, I can do that.

That's about the point in my life where I became unable to do anything. His producer kept calling and leaving messages. Surely Albert Maysles can tell when there's a junkie at his dinner table? But the producer kept calling.

I don't remember a word of conversation, but I have a fantasy that Albert Maysles saw something in me that was worth coaxing from the brink. After I got clean, I was too ashamed to call. He died in 2015.

NARROW (1988, 1992, 2001)

_____ went to Sarah Lawrence. Her bed was as narrow as a convict's bunk. When I visited, we slept on the floor.

Her roommate slept in the other bed—what, like she'd crash in someone else's room? She played her falling-asleep mixtape, which she'd copied from a friend, who'd dubbed it off a friend. A third-hand copy, tape of a tape of a tape. The hiss was like wind on the tundra.

First three songs: Paul Simon, "Slip Slidin' Away," X, "See How We Are," Natalie Merchant and Tracy Chapman singing "Where the Soul Never Dies" as a hypnotic round.

I didn't know these songs, and _____'s roommate hadn't copied the track list. But I knew Paul Simon's voice; I'd seen _See How We Are_ in the bins; I recognized Natalie Merchant and Tracy Chapman.

The fourth song was like a miniature: a soft guitar—palm muting, that _chrmmm-chrmmm-chrmmm_—a softly grieving synth, a soft, plain voice. There was no chorus.

The first line was: _When the rich die last, like the rabbits running._

The last line was: _There is peace outside in the narrow light._

She sang as if at midnight with someone asleep in the next room.

The world was absolutely new.

I begged for the tape. I went looking for the friend with the dual-tape box, but she was gone for the weekend. Who's got the original? Someone at her high school.

That night _____'s friends drank schnapps and played Wing-span; girls on either side of another girl lifted her hair, which was measured point to point. They played it all the time, but the winners never changed.

Someone was documenting the wingspans with a camcorder and turned the lens on me; I said, If you ever have a kid who wants to know what you were like in college, you can go, Hey, kid, watch this!

I meant it to sound ridiculous, and it did, because we would be who we were that night forever, or until Reagan started a nuclear war.

Not that we really thought so. But, really, we thought so.

I begged _____'s roommate to let me take the tape. I have a dual deck, I'll copy it! You'll get it back!

I rode the Metro-North listening to the *narrow light* song over and over again. Click, rewind, no that's too far, click, fast-forward, play. It's a short song.

An exasperated man with his briefcase in his lap became enraged. "What is this clicking?! What is this clicking?!"

At home I copied the mixtape: a tape of a tape of a tape of a tape.

Later I made a new mix for myself and put it on there: tape of a tape of a tape of a tape of a tape. The song was so brief that I was disappointed when it ended, so I put it on the mixtape twice in a row.

I hooked up a VCR to the tape deck and—between songs—recorded dialogue snippets from the original Pee-wee Herman HBO special: *Say hello to my hypnosis doll, Dr. Mondo!*

I listened for years to the *narrow light* song and never knew who it was or what it was called.

I heard a band play the song at the Knitting Factory. *Oh my god it's them!*

I heard it emanating from the performance space upstairs; I couldn't leave the doorman's desk. It was during New Music Seminar, so there were eight bands on the bill; which one was this?!

I found the singer and buttonholed her. "Oh—that's not our song. I don't know—the guitar player showed me." The rest of her band had left.

Cut to the invention of the search engine and iTunes: I'd only owned the song on mixtapes, and one day I remembered it. What was that song?

It's "Final Day," released in 1980, by the Welsh band Young Marble Giants.

It was a band name I'd seen, as I had seen so, so many bands' names. What else was on the albums I saw in the bins and didn't buy?

CENT (1983)

A seventh-grade friend—incidentally, now in the FBI—repeatedly cheated the Columbia Record & Tape Club. The Columbia Record & Tape Club ran clip-out ads in *Circus* and *Hit Parader*, which said *Ten Albums for One Cent!*

There was a circle on the form that said *Tape Penny Here.*

You sent your penny with a list of selections. You were then required to buy a certain number of albums—picking them from a monthly Columbia Record & Tape Club pamphlet, writing the serial numbers on a postcard—within a year. So the albums weren't really a penny.

The real hustle was that they'd mail you an album every month if you didn't send in a postcard declining it. If you did decline, you'd get a threatening postcard saying how many you were still on the hook for. If you forgot, the album showed up on your doorstep and you owed them $8.98.

Because of this, my friends—metal kids all—had Lionel Richie and Sheena Easton albums among their Dokken and Ratt.

We feared the long arm of the Columbia Record & Tape Club. But my friend just kept sending the pennies, getting his ten albums, throwing away the unwanted records. He used pseudonyms, but not a dummy address—the Columbia Record & Tape Club didn't cross-reference addresses for deadbeats.

None of us were brave enough to take up his game.

One of the names he used was Harry Truman. There was something about the 1980s that suited people named Harry Truman who weren't the Missouri-born thirty-third president of the United

States. There was Sheriff Harry Truman on *Twin Peaks*; there was an eighty-three-year-old man named Harry Truman who lived in a lodge on a lake at the foot of Mount St. Helens and refused to move when the mountain became volcanically active. He was presumed to have been immolated by hot gas and volcanic matter when Mount St. Helens erupted on May 18, 1980.

ARE YOU FROM ENGLAND?
(2002)

I heard an urban legend that Little Richard lived in the penthouse at the Hyatt House on Sunset Boulevard. They called it the Riot House in the '70s, when all bands stayed there. It was where Robert Plant stood on a balcony, gazed at Los Angeles, and yelled, "I am a golden god!"

I got in the elevator, and there was Little Richard.

It was not an urban legend.

He wore a suit like the dancers in Janet Jackson's "Rhythm Nation" video. His face was flawlessly smoothed with foundation; his lips and his eyes were lined; his black curls shone. A floral scent billowed profusely.

"Are you from *England*?" he asked me.

No, from New York, same deal right ha ha?

"Hmm!" he puffed, and closed his eyes.

MIMED CUFFS (1991)

My roommate and I left a party at a girl's place and went down into the Twenty-Third Street station to get the C train.

A gate was held open with string. Come on, let's walk through! Saving $1.15 was meaningful to me.

Cops came from nowhere. One was wearing a dirty beige Members Only jacket. The other guy had an American-flag bandanna on his head. They handcuffed us.

My roommate had his token in his hand as they handcuffed him. "Take it! Please take it!"

They led us down to a storage room. There were actual rooms behind those doors on the platform? They sat us among mops, with two glum dudes.

We waited an hour, then they paraded us up the stairs. Everyone gawking, *What did they do?*

There was a corrections department bus parked at the entrance.

A cop came close to me. "If you've got drugs just give them to me now, just give them to me now."

Mine were long gone. My roommate had a razor blade in his wallet, which he used to cut things out of newspapers. The cop took it. But it was true!

There were only the four of us on the bus. My roommate and I struggled to sit with our hands cuffed behind our backs. The other two dudes had the hang of it.

My roommate was glaring at me. He had multiple auditions the next day.

They led us down into the Canal Street station—we drove from one stop on the C train to another stop on the C train. There was a police station down there.

They put us in a holding cell, the four guys, took our names, fingerprinted us. The cops kept making jokes about jacking off. Not cruel jokes, just work-tedium jokes.

The lack of animus was the most surreal thing about being there—given how afraid I was.

One asked me what I did. I told him I reviewed CDs for the *NYPress*.

"You make a lot of money doing that?"

I had a Pennsylvania license—I got it when my dad was living down there. "Pennsylvania? Why'd you move to this shithole?"

One of the cops said, "We just do this to check if people have warrants on them."

One of the other two dudes did have a warrant.

We got out at three in the morning with pieces of paper pertaining to our hearings, signed by our arresting officers. Mine, it turned out, was Officer Evan J. Smelley.

I told Strausbaugh about it—to me it was a numb tale of stupidity, but he was fascinated. He made me write it up. They ran it with a rather accurate illustration: ungovernable blond hair and absurdly baggy pants.

At the hearing we watched person after person go in front of the judge for fare evasion. She would half-squeal a sentence of community service or a fine. No discernable logic as to who got which.

Everybody stood with their hands held behind their back, as if they were handcuffed. But what else would you do? Put them in your pockets? Fold your arms?

A lawyer found me. She was walking up and down the aisles saying her clients' names; she took them into the hall for a few minutes, then they'd go in front of the judge and be sentenced.

I had a copy of *NYPress*.

"Oh, this is—wow. Okay. I've never had one of these before."

She held it up when we were in front of the judge. The DA said something along the lines of *This is injustice, we call for an investigation.*

"They don't really care," said my lawyer—whom I'd met ten minutes ago—when it was done.

I got a call from the cops. I was high. "How did you get this number??"

Pause. "You're listed."

The cop went through the article, asking me about every single curse word—if the cop had said it. "Is it true that the officer said, 'What the fuck are you doing, asshole?' Is it true that the officer said, 'Put your dick away, you piece of shit?'"

These were things they said *to each other.* Cops couldn't be quoted cursing in newspapers.

I got a call to be on *Leonard Lopate.*

I was on the show with someone from the MTA. He wore a brown three-piece suit. He looked like the guy in Tommy Tutone, but squatter, and with a severe part in his hair.

I think I was wearing my William S. Burroughs shirt.

A button in front of my mic said *COUGH.* What does this do?

"A little hand comes out and grabs your testicles," said Leonard Lopate.

I didn't laugh *at all.* It was like a negative laugh.

I was extremely, extremely nervous, and now Leonard Lopate thought I was some grimy white punk out to make him feel old and unfunny.

The MTA guy opened a briefcase and took out papers; he read statistics about how much money is lost to people who jump turnstiles. Was I here to debate him?

I remember saying it was like being in a Mamet play, which I don't think is what they expected from the fare-evading kid. I didn't think there was anything unusual or unjust about what happened to me.

I didn't jump the turnstile, I said. I just walked through. The cop told me they strung the door open because they wanted to check if people had warrants.

"No no no," said Leonard Lopate. "That would be *unconstitutional*."

CARRYING (2016)

Somebody told me there's money in house tours. There isn't—not exceptionally—and the worst house shows are the worst shows. But the best house shows are uniquely great. No mic, no speakers: you're playing into shared air.

The intensity was overwhelming. For a dozen shows I stayed mum between songs; I could barely manage to apologize for the lack of banter. Eventually I realized that banter was part of the draw—regular fans were appalled—so I forced myself. I sounded like a kid at a talent show killing time while the bass player tunes up.

There are companies who specialize in finding the hosts, who don't get anything out of it except a free show. They have the responsibility of checking names off at their door. The artist is sent a list of hosts beforehand, to check for stalkers.

Key prerequisites are the sizes of the living rooms and availability of parking; I discovered mid-tour that this meant the hosts are rich. I do my best to shut down my stupid mind when somebody else's wealth makes me stupidly feel bad. But I would pull up to a palace and question my life.

We were in a minivan, and all we had were two guitars, two boxes of merch, me, Scrap, and a merch person, Jack Slattery Dream Husband. We'd pull up and there would be dudes with beers waiting on the lawn—like they're in a crow's nest watching for icebergs. Staring unnervingly—visibly freaked out.

Jack Slattery Dream Husband would jump out, his hands spread like you're supposed to do when confronting mountain lions. The dudes would crowd the minivan. Do you need help?? Do you need help?? Can I carry something?? Do you need help??

Why is it unsettling? It's dudes who want to carry boxes.

But it is.

Scrap couldn't look up while we played the shows. "They look like the people in 'Black Hole Sun,' man."

Meaning cartoonishly huge eyes, like in the Soundgarden video.

My audience are largely dudes who were Soul Coughing fans in high school; a lot of them look exactly like me: shaved heads, glasses. It's like the scene in *Ladies and Gentlemen, the Fabulous Stains* where they play in a mall, escalators packed with girls dressed exactly like Diane Lane, with the skunk hair, sheer red blouses, eyes painted as flames.

SNAKE PEOPLE

Fans my age came up to the merch table and complained—as if Jack Slattery Dream Husband were the customer service department—that I shouldn't use drum machines on my records.

It's like the fear that cameras steal your soul.

When he expressed disbelief that anybody could be so old-fashioned as to think drum machines weren't musical instruments, I smiled and said, Whatever, snake person.

There was a Chrome extension that converted *millennials* to *snake people*:

Snake People Killing the Movie Business
Why Are Snake People Killing Their Bosses?
"Promiscuous" Snake People Killing McDonald's
Did Snake People Kill Hangout Sitcoms?

ORIGIN STORIES

Dudes tell me their Soul Coughing origin stories. I'm not good at it.

The stories are like:

"When I was in college, me and my buddies took a road trip to Pittsburgh . . ."

Or:

"I took a bunch of mushrooms at my friend's house . . ."

Long stories: plot reversals, secondary characters, golden sunrises at the denouements. They end with something like " . . . and then I heard 'Super Bon Bon' on the radio."

I want, desperately, to be kind, but I have no poker face. Some dudes, if they feel my response is unenthusiastic, repeat their story. If it's a very drunk dude (they always wait to be last), I say, "Please tell me your story in one sentence."

The one-sentence version is usually like, "My roommate had the CD."

Scrap and I riff about it: *I escaped from a gulag and lived on wolves' corpses for three years—I found my way to the Arctic—I floated on ice for a hundred miles—I was rescued by the Canadian navy—they brought me to Tahiti, where I became a carpenter—and then "Circles" was playing in a bar.*

Or: *I sought the elimination of my ego, so I abandoned my life—I attained ineffability and floated through the ether—my essence re-formed as a dragon—a band of hunters fired on me with shotguns—in dirt, I scratched DO NOT KILL ME FOR I HAVE*

THE SOUL OF A MAN—*and then I saw the video for "Circles" right after Len's "Steal My Sunshine."*

It's my job to receive the stories; to show the fan that I see them, and hear them; to help them make a story about the time I met them and they told me their story. It's not about me, it's not about me, it's not about me.

HORNET

I got groped in Charlotte by a guy in a Hornets jersey. It was his house. He was wasted and kept yelling things at me from his sofa during the show.

His wife wore a stylish dress. She sat next to him, occasionally trying to quiet him by patting his jorted leg and kissing his chin-bearded face.

That kind of beard that just delineates where the fat stops: the chindicator.

After the show, he wanted a picture; he drunkenly insisted she be in it. The mortified wife on one side, the guy in the Hornets jersey on the other.

His hand reached out and massaged my side creepily—grabbed a hunk of pudge and squeezed it.

I barked and ran out.

"But I'm a very comfortable person!" he yelled after me.

SEMI-HOLLOW (1994)

I walked into 48th Street Custom Guitars with money from Warner Bros. to buy gear. I blew it all on one guitar: a 1968 Fender Coronado II, painted an extraordinary shade of green. A semi-hollow, from what they called the Wildwood series: they injected colored dye into living beech trees.

It was a hassle to play. The strings popped out if you thwacked them wrong, which I always did—and do. The bridge is held to the instrument by tension, so if you change the strings you have to jimmy it back into place.

The Coronado was a failed model. Fender was trying to compete with Guild, Rickenbacker, the Gibson ES-335—all the hollow-body and semi-hollow-body guitars that the Beatles made fashionable in the 1960s—so they made this janky thing that I now had in my hands.

COOLER (1994, 1996, 1998)

The first time I played the green Coronado was at the Cooler, a basement club in the Meatpacking District.

The weird string issues fucked me up.

I still look at the guitar and see that club.

It used to be a meat locker. There was a track along the ceiling where the carcasses hung—pushed down the line as they were hacked. It was highly designed, with curvy furniture; the walls were painted an unpropitious lavender. It was owned by a guy named Jedi, a sad sack who'd invite bands to get high in his office.

Bands declined: Jedi freaked us out. Nobody seemed to know anything about where he came from—rich family? We speculated: Did he sink his riches into a club so he could get high with bands?

When Soul Coughing had put records out and was playing Irving Plaza, I went to the Cooler to see Clean Girls. Jedi was bitter that I'd abandoned him.

Irving Plaza fits fifteen hundred people, I said.

"We can fit fifteen hundred people in here!" said Jedi peevishly.

Wait. Are you really telling me this?

"Yes, absolutely you could get that many people in here."

Jedi. Fifteen hundred. One five zero zero. Look at this place.

"Of course we could," he said, gawping at me like I was gaslighting him.

When Giuliani declared vindictive war on *quality-of-life offenses*, using the cabaret laws to issue outrageous fines and shut clubs down, the Cooler installed a switch at the doorman's station that turned the house lights on full blast and cut the sound system. If cops showed up, the switch was flipped and the fun stopped.

It was justified: cops closed bars if they saw somebody dance— any bar, any dancing. All bar employees were perceptibly paranoid. Lone goofballs and drunk girls got bounced for prancing.

Meat was still being packed in the Meatpacking District. At night the neighborhood was so deserted that packs of trans hookers stood in the middle of Eighth Avenue. They had screaming matches with boys from Jersey who shouted insults from moving cars. On frigid nights, the trans hookers repaired—in shifts—to Dizzy Izzy's Bagels and drank coffee from *We Are Happy to Serve You* cups. They sat among workers wearing bloodied white coats.

FIXES (1995)

I played an ugly purple Yamaha instead of the exasperating Coronado. I'd bought it from an NYU kid who'd played it in his high school hardcore bands. It's the kind of guitar your dad buys if he thinks you're wasting your time.

I was embarrassed to have blown so much dough on a guitar I didn't play, and even more embarrassed to have a record deal but be playing this Yamaha. I jerry-rigged a solution: I put a capo on the Coronado's nut—the piece of plastic between a guitar's neck and head—to keep the strings in place.

When Soul Coughing could afford a stage crew, confident guitar techs would tell me that they could adjust the bridge just so, or shave down a tiny bit into the plastic of the nut: just trust them.

It never worked. I still play it, decades later, with the capo on there to keep the strings from popping out.

COMPLIMENT (1998)

I played "Circles" with Soul Coughing on *Late Night* in 1998. David Letterman walked over afterward, as he does, to shake the singer's hand—pleasantries semi-audible to the TV audience—as the show cuts to commercial.

He pointed to the green Coronado and said, "That's a beautiful guitar!"

I blurted, You're a great American poet!

He fake-laughed a very David Letterman fake laugh, forbidding and shallow, that was like "Weh-he-he-he-ell!" and bolted.

What a shitty thing to do to the guy. I did a thing that people do to me all the time: essentially saying, *You made a thing that changed my life, now I want you to thank me for it.*

I felt stupid, but having my guitar complimented by David Letterman was a life accomplishment.

COMPLIMENTS (2013)

My drummer Pete Wilhoit said that David Letterman had complimented his drums: "He does that thing, you know, where he compliments drums." He does?

Pete typed *letterman compliment drums* into YouTube; there was a six-minute compilation: "Those are some nice drums!" [cut] "Where'd you get those drums?" [cut] "That's a good-looking set of drums there!"

I typed *letterman compliment guitar* and found: "That's a beautiful guitar!" [cut] "Hey, can I have that guitar?" [cut] "That guitar looks great!"

But maybe it was a great thing to have been part of a recurring Letterman motif. Then I thought, *I didn't even make the YouTube reel.*

RECKLESSNESSES (2018)

I come out of the brutal Memphis summer looking like a cave dweller, having spent months huddling by a central-cooling vent. On the first exquisite autumn day, I opened every window in the house and inadvertently left one open overnight.

A crash woke me up; my chihuahua, Lunchy, went apeshit.

That dumb shelf, I thought.

I went back to sleep.

The next day I found that the screen had disappeared from a wide-open window in the studio. I figured the wind dislodged it.

I worked on some poems; I read the *Times* on my phone; I messed around with a drum machine I'd bought on eBay—a pedal from the 1970s, marketed explicitly to guitar players with no friends. Lunchy was being a dick, so I took him to daycare, where he could be a dick to other dogs.

When I got back, I sat down to switch the computer on and noticed that the left speaker wasn't there.

After a moment trying to remember when I'd unplugged a speaker and put it in a different room, I realized I'd been robbed. The thieves had taken that cheap speaker—only the left speaker—a cheap mic, a cheap mic stand, and the two most expensive guitars I owned.

I like cheap guitars. They suit me. I've got a dozen of them. The two that got stolen were the only valuable instruments I have. The kids probably didn't know; they just took the shiny ones.

One was a National Reso-Lectric, and the other was the Coronado—neither irreplaceable nor, in relative terms, particularly expensive, but

I'd paid extra insurance and listed its value as $25,000. Nobody selling that guitar could get anything like $25,000 for it, but it would be—it was—a huge loss. If I do a show without it, people tell me they're disappointed not to have seen the green guitar.

The cops asked for pictures: I typed *Soul Coughing* into Google and showed them screenshots of me playing it on *Letterman*. I emphasized, repeatedly, that nobody could sell it for what it was insured for, but a cop told me that its insured value obliged them to have a guy come dust for fingerprints.

It wasn't an ingenious heist. I'd left my window wide open.

They asked me what the serial number was—pawnshops are required to run the serial number. I had to tell them that, in the quarter century I'd owned this guitar, I never wrote down the serial number.

I put up a screenshot on Instagram, with a plea for people to be on the lookout. A friend of mine texted, *I have a good feeling about this. You're going to get it back.*

I spent the day going to pawnshops, showing them pictures, and hearing every time, "That's gorgeous. Do you have the serial number?"

A week later, a detective called and said, "You're not going to believe this."

He said he'd love to take credit, but it was a fluke: they picked up two kids for breaking into a car, one of them thirteen and the other sixteen; the sixteen-year-old grassed on the thirteen-year-old, saying it wasn't his idea and he could tell the cops where some guitars were.

The cop said the thirteen-year-old was the bold one; the sixteen-year-old just went along with it. It fascinated me that a sixteen-year-old would be friends with—and intimidated into participating in the crimes of—a younger kid. He told me they'd intended to steal more but were frightened by the barking of my dog—a seven-pound chihuahua.

I got the cheap mic, cheap stand, cheap speaker back, too.

I gave the cops a statement, which was that I'd heard a crash and seen nothing. And what's the value again? I told him it depended on who was selling it, and to whom.

The cop pressed me—come on, it's not the resale price that makes it valuable.

I wondered if he was trying to jack up the charges on the two kids.

I wrote my sympathetic friend: *Thank you for your kind prescience.*

Oh, he texted back. *I was just saying that. I figured that guitar was gone forever.*

The city sent a form letter: the thieves were to go in front of a judge that day. The hearing was at 9 a.m. and the mail came at 4 p.m., so I'd missed it. They had names that could be stereotyped as African American.

As a kid, I was like that sixteen-year-old—I always had friends like his. If we found an open window, I would've reluctantly helped my friend rob a house. Bad white kids rarely have to answer for their recklessnesses.

IN AN ELEVATOR (1990)

An old man who'd been in the folk scene in Greenwich Village—in the 1960s, when it wasn't the *West* Village yet—started telling me stories about Dave Van Ronk and Joan Baez. He wore tinted glasses and an ascot. An ascot!

It was fascinating for a moment, but then it became like he was pulling my collar and punching my face with words. I was barely out of my teens and hadn't developed much empathy. He had all this bottled up, and nobody to tell it to. I recoiled from his age, the way a young person does.

IN AN ELEVATOR (1991)

The doors opened; there were two guys with rubber gloves pushing a gurney.

One of them said, "We're funeral directors?"

He indicated somehow that I should get off the elevator.

I did. I stood in the hallway with a young guy, who was staring at the elevator doors with a kind of embarrassed sorrow.

I wondered about it for a long time: they had learned that it's best they ride alone, because they have a corpse, was to say, *We're funeral directors?* Is it improper to be on an elevator with a body? Were they trying to avoid somebody realizing, in horror, that they were riding with the dead? Is there somebody who was insulted, and refused to get out?

IN AN ELEVATOR (1992)

I was blasting my knockoff Walkman. One of the foam ear-
phone covers was missing and the jack was half-busted, so I had to
keep my thumb on it or the left channel would buzz out.

A guy in his forties, not an egregiously I'm-groovy dad, more
like a *Voice*-reader dad, got on and heard the hissing from the
earphones.

He said, "What are you listening to?"

The Jackson 5, I told him.

"Really??" he said, beaming.

VENTILATION (2014)

I got a commission to write an opera based on the Book of Revelation, so I rented a studio to compose in: it was on Stanhope Street, on the same block as a Hindu temple.

It was a warren of subdivided rehearsal holes with bands crammed in them. Once my amps and guitars were in, there was a three-foot aperture that fit a single chair.

The rule of rehearsal studios is that there is always a metal band on one side and on the other a drummer who can play many, many, many notes really, really, really fast.

So I worked early mornings.

I'd be walking in as bleary kids—edgy because the coke ran out—were dumping their beer cans into the trash baskets. It seemed proper: the middle-aged artist says good morning to young artists who say good night.

The guy who managed the place was a sandy-blond kid from Pocatello who, for his labor, was given a windowless cubby slightly larger than a mattress. He sat in the hall with a half-busted Dell laptop and an overflowing ashtray.

I asked him why he was in the hall; he told me the ventilation was better.

I told him that I couldn't live without a window.

He indulgently explained *that's how it is in New York*.

What do I know? I've only been here *since the '80s*.

His friends also lived in windowless cubbies. My people lived among menacing derelicts, but we had windows. We coped with danger; they cope with humiliation.

MASSACHUSETTS TROOPERS
IN JAPANESE CARS (1986)

I had a drummer friend named J. Why?. He wore *London Calling* shirts with the sleeves cut off and had this beautiful hair: part fade, part mullet. Like an Art Deco hedge. One dreadlocked strand fell from the back.

He was seventeen, I was sixteen. We had a band first called the Difference, and then Dada Dred, playing the snack bar at our school in exchange for grilled cheeses with sprouts.

We took his blue Volvo to Boston, down the Mass Pike: his sister Hillary went to BU. I think he had alcoholics in his family, so he didn't get high. But I did.

He drove dumb fast, like a seventeen-year-old does.

I was looking at cars, saying, That's a cop that's a cop that's a cop.

"That's a Toyota. Cops drive Crown Victorias. Not cars *from Japan*."

We listened to Run-DMC's *Raising Hell* twice, letting the tape auto-reverse.

Hillary got us tickets to *Blue Velvet* with money her mom gave her for cultural expenses—they'd just had a fight because her mom meant the ballet, not *movies*.

I owned an *Eraserhead* T-shirt, but hadn't seen the movie. I wore the shirt to Disneyland and got a photo with Mickey Mouse.

We crashed on her dorm-room floor. She had a gorgeous roommate, with blue-black bangs cut severely over her eyes. They had TV, which we did not have at our school. I felt too ashamed to turn it on: I'd absorbed the superiority of arty-hippie-wealthy New England kids.

The next day I saw a girl dressed all in black, with Malcolm X glasses, skateboarding down Commonwealth Avenue. Just getting to class, not doing tricks. She had a fat sketchbook tucked under her arm. I was in awe.

J. Why? and his sister had a band in high school; she'd been in love with the guitar player about whom she wrote songs—which he obliviously played, alongside covers of "Brand New Cadillac" and "Sunday Bloody Sunday."

Don't you know you're the king of my fantasyland? the lyrics of one went.

Hillary now loved the bass player in a band called Baldo Rex. She'd been the only person standing in front at their T.T. the Bear's show.

She dragged us to their rehearsal, in a shoddy complex of plywood cubicles—unheated, strewn with trash. The amps had salt stains from sweaty bands. They'd made a map of New York out of bottles: Manhattan outlined in Rolling Rock, Absolut for the Empire State Building.

They played a song called "Carbon Demon Bologna Spaceship." They would act like they were rocking a massive room, then suddenly see the sad group of younger teenagers sitting on the floor in front of them.

They took a beer break. Hillary, J. Why?, and I took up their instruments; we hacked through the easy part of "Sweet Jane." I played bass and sang. I discovered that I couldn't play the riff and sing at the same time.

I played a simple *bmm bmm bmm bmm* on the lowest string, periodically shifting a clumsy finger to the A: it worked. It was "Sweet Jane." I actually thought I sounded better than when the bass and guitar played the riff together.

The world was absolutely new.

BILLS, BEARS (1994)

When Soul Coughing got our first CD, we found a baffling line after the PO box for fan mail: *AOL: Soulcghng*

Our manager explained: the future.

I went to the chat rooms using the login. A plurality of the chat rooms were named *Friends of Bill W* or *Bears 4 Bears*. I didn't know what either meant.

I was in a chat room called *Auto Pimp*, after a Future Sound of London track. Somebody typed, *hey ashley nice screen name.*

I told him I was *in* Soul Coughing. I told him to get his CD and look in the booklet and he'd see my screen name. A few minutes passed.

holy fuck no way, he typed.

STEALTH HEDDAS

I found a Soul Coughing message board: just a few posts, most expressing surprise that Soul Coughing warranted a message board. What AOL employee decided which bands would get them? Warner Bros. didn't call AOL to demand it.

Among the posts was the first shot at viral marketing I ever saw: *anybody heard portishead's dummy? great ear candy.* The same screen name had posted the same post, verbatim, on other bands' boards.

I never saw one of those for any band on AOL again.

Our video got onto *120 Minutes*—the second-to-last video, around 1:50 a.m., introduced by Lewis Largent with, "What's up with all the New York bands tonight?"

Nobody knew what we looked like. Somebody posted, *i can't believe the voice of soul coughing comes from THAT.*

Not only did it emotionally destroy me, but Warner Bros. received the board's feedback as grimly as it would rejection from MTV itself. They saw message boards as prognosticators—flocks of ghostly Hedda Hoppers.

Around the time when AOL bought Time Warner—obviously, their parent—Warner Bros. transitioned their bands onto websites, each with a BBS.

There was much attention paid to the Dead's ethos: the principles of the parking lot. It was advantageous—moral, even—to encourage a little society to accumulate next to a band. But people on a BBS weren't like Deadheads: they were people who built a little clubhouse next to your tour dates. They were killing time at work.

Complex hierarchies developed among regular posters; inside jokes; behavioral conventions. Strangers could post band questions and be shunned as *Ausländer*.

All the bands were quietly freaked out that their fans weren't that interested in them—they may as well have united under the banner of cheeseburgers or macramé.

YOU MUST EARN THE SHIRT (1986)

J. Why? and I went to Harvard Square to see buskers. It was late September. There was a soft breeze; it felt like the world loved us for once.

I expected to hear devastating musical forces on every corner.

I heard a drums-and-guitar duo doing wobbly Stones covers. They were called Wicked Bizarre. Say that band name in your worst imitation of a Boston accent.

Two crusty kids banged tandem marimbas on Brattle Street. One wore a black Replacements shirt. It was the exact Replacements shirt I'd always wanted: the cover of *Let It Be* on a black shirt!—with them pictured on a roof, wearing jeans and smoking.

It was before I could enjoy Indonesian music, or weird Harry Partch stuff, or Steve Reich's *Music for 18 Musicians*. I couldn't abide a disconnect between the marimba and the Replacements.

Did the marimba player earn this shirt? I dreamed of finding his shirt at White Knight Records. I hated my own Replacements shirt, which was the cover of *Tim* screen-printed in hot pink.

Hot pink! I didn't want to wear it, but the Replacements were my everything, and those are the rules.

MINGER (2003)

Unbeknownst to them, Friendster invented the profile. It was conceived as a dating site: your page was friends' testimonials. The friend who invited me—she had a three-digit user number!—wrote of me, *My eyes explode with liquid love!*

Everybody who didn't work at a web company had a dial-up modem. They were suddenly jammed: nobody could get on. There were a few weeks in which it seemed the whole world was obsessively refreshing their browsers, desperate to get to Friendster.

Friendster took it as a violation, deleting profiles that were flagrantly unrelated to dating.

There was a guy on there called Minger: a guy in a black T-shirt, emo swoop over his eye, holding up a fist, like, *Yeah, buddy!*

He had thousands of friends. It became a thing. "You're friends with Minger, too? Do you know him?"

Everybody thought they must have a friend who was Minger's *actual* friend.

Friendster deleted him; he reappeared, re-accumulating his legion at wild speed. Every time they kicked him off, a new Minger would appear and quickly recoup—plus thousands more. He'd post that Friendster couldn't stop him.

MySpace arrived—built to obsolesce Friendster.

Friendster's founder appeared on *Charlie Rose*, boasting that they'd seen this world coming. No mention of dating.

I looked at Friendster before I typed this. The page says *Friendster came about through an enduring passion to make a difference.*

I looked up *minger* and found hundreds of faces but no Minger.

I've wondered if Minger named himself after Mingering Mike, a fake recording artist: the fantasy of a guy in DC who drew pretend record covers, found decades later in thrift stores. There have been museum shows and art books. Over thirty albums and forty singles have been found. Among them: *Channels of a Dream*, *From Our Mind to Yours*, and *The Two Sides of Mingering Mike*.

VAN (1990)

I had a job delivering ice cream in a beat-up Dodge Ram. Delivering to restaurants. I lie by omission and say I drove an ice-cream van.

The company's thing was high-end gelato, but their money came from making green tea and red bean ice cream for Japanese restaurants—an unusual number of which were, independently, named Ichiban. We had running jokes about how disgusting we found green tea and red bean.

It was on Broome Street, across from a storefront psychic and a Puerto Rican diner called Brisas del Caribe. Every night the street was choked with cars headed into the Holland Tunnel.

The owners were two yuppie guys—business school friends— who bought the place when looking for a business they could pump up and sell off: business school moves. One of them was a handsome man, very tall, with prematurely thinning blond hair, who became possessed by Lisa Stansfield's "All Around the World" and power walked to Tower Records—eight blocks up Broadway—came back with the cassingle, and blasted it over and over.

The other guy, a short guy, was a bona fide WASP who went by his initials: not a normal initials name, like D.J. or J.J., but like R.M. or Q.W.—something you could envision on a portrait over a fireplace in a wood-paneled den.

I was on the stoop, scrutinizing a map. *Park Slope, where is that? Is that where Maureen's mom lives? No, Maureen's mom lives in . . . what is that neighborhood called again?*

So it was 1990.

I saw a hand reach for my sunglasses, which were on the steps next to me. I'd bought them at a stand on Broadway: cheap plastic lenses, with a bootleg UV-safe sticker. I tried to grab them—a reflex— but the hand flicked mine away, and he pushed me back onto the step. This huge, aggro man.

"Do you want to buy them back?"

Do I want to buy them back. No, I don't want to buy them back. They're four dollars on the corner.

Not that I was an endless fount of four dollars.

Out of the store came R.M. or Q.W. "What's going on here?" He got the vibe.

"Well," said R.M. or Q.W., a scrawny dude, trying to save face in front of the aggro man. "Okay, well."

His tone was something like: *You boys settle your disagreement while I attend to an important matter.* He hurried back into the store.

It seemed to dawn on the guy that he had gone to the trouble of rolling somebody for something worthless. But he couldn't take a mulligan and hand them back. He put the cheap sunglasses on. They made his head look very fat. He walked away.

NEAR ELLENSBURG (2004)

I was out with a trio: myself; a very delicate, Chopin-loving piano player; and a drummer who was constantly on a coarse-grind hustle. If you had to reimburse him for a cab, it turned out he had to go to Staten Island, could we do cash? He had gotten his first cell phone but for some reason it was never charged and he had to borrow yours. He didn't need his $25 per diem, could you just pay for these groceries? Naturally $40 worth of groceries.

He was an actual person whose voicemail started with, "Hi, how are you?" Pause. Pause. "Thanks for calling! Please leave a message."

I couldn't look at him.

We were driving from Boise to Seattle. Near Ellensburg, in those oscillating yellow hills. The piano player had an old iPod: it had actual buttons that clicked. The white was now dirty ivory.

He put on Steve Reich's *Music for 18 Musicians*.

It was like those undulant marimbas rose from the yellow hills. The melodies change as if you're passing them: a note materializes at the end, a note on the top disappears. It's an Ouroboros.

Has anyone heard it for the first time anywhere but in a moving car on an interstate, watching blond grasslands turn into pine trees?

The world was absolutely new.

JUST ONE TOUCH
AND BABY I BELIEVE (2010)

We were on the Jackie Robinson Parkway in Scrap's Toyota. We were listening to Z-100; Scrap is one of the few people who don't think I listen to pop radio as a means of trolling. Katy Perry's "Teenage Dream" came on.

I forgot about the song until I was on the Q train; I realized I didn't have it on my phone. The stretch over the Manhattan Bridge— between DeKalb in Brooklyn and Canal Street in Manhattan— is the longest distance between stops in the entire New York subway system. I rushed to open iTunes and download it. Barely nabbed it before the train was underground again.

I was going to *The 24 Hour Plays* on Broadway—I was the musical guest that year. Sometimes the directors put the musicians in the plays (one-acts written over one night, staged the next); I was in one doing a version of "Rock-a-Bye Baby" (Julianna Margulies asked if I gave lessons, I said I don't, really—and so I turned down the opportunity to go to Julianna Margulies's house and bond over Led Zeppelin riffs), and in another as a musician hired by Sam Rockwell to play while he wooed Naomi Watts.

I wandered around Times Square, listening to "Teenage Dream" over and over again. It's such a tragic lyric: from the outside, it's all skin-tight jeans and triumphant joyrides. But it's not about gleeful teens: it's about drunks just about to turn thirty.

That gleaming production and the soaring Max Martin melody. The crowds were shadows under the neon of the gigantic Bank of America sign.

The world was absolutely new.

In the Sam Rockwell play, he's rejected by Naomi Watts and goes offstage. Mid-play, I was standing behind the curtain with Sam Rockwell, *who was still acting*. He's incredible.

I fucked it up: I thought I was supposed to do something, so I said, I'm really sorry to bring this up, but you still have to pay me.

It was like I was alone with Eddie Van Halen and jumped in with half-assed blues licks.

We came back onstage for him to re-woo her; I was to jam with Fisher Stevens, who played harmonica. Sam Rockwell entreated Naomi Watts wordlessly, with his back to the audience. Nobody saw that performance but me.

The after-party was at B.B. King's—sixty feet west of the theater. I was walking out the glass doors in front and was grabbed by a producer. "Come with us!"

I got pulled into a scrum surrounding Jennifer Aniston. We were circled by photographers—ugly, sloppy men—yelling foul provocations. We were the nucleus and they were in hideous orbit. We walked with painful slowness, the pace of pilgrims crawling on their bellies to a shrine.

EON (2000)

I got a call from somebody at a groovy box-set company; they'd acquired the Warner Bros. catalog. Or Warner Bros. acquired them?

She asked if I'd be interested in doing a Soul Coughing best-of. There's only three albums: it would be odd. Thanks, goodbye.

She called the next day to clarify: they *were going to do* a Soul Coughing best-of.

She said her boss told her to pick a band from the Warner Bros. stack. Anything she liked. She'd been an assistant; this was a promotion.

She sent a track list: almost entirely songs from our first album, *Ruby Vroom*.

Very cool, thanks, but if it's a compilation, we could cover all three albums, and some soundtracks?

"But those are the best songs," she said.

She wanted to call it *Paleolithic Eon*—a lyric from the song "Sugar Free Jazz."

I heard it as *fossilized*.

"But, no, let me send you this graphic I had our designer do. The way those words look together."

No, I really don't like it. No—you don't have to send—no, seriously, I've made up my—no.

I agreed to write liner notes—reluctantly—if they agreed not to run them past my ex-bandmates. Soul Coughing was wall-to-wall opposition: when I'd suggest something, they'd become enraged and insist on the opposite. They'd cut their own jugulars and hope I bled to death.

I offered to bow out. Terrifying, because my ex-bandmates' stories disincluded me: they'd told interviewers that they'd already been a band, playing shows in clubs, and I was a random kid who begged to join.

Who were they gaslighting? Themselves?

One had a MySpace with pictures of other artists we'd worked with—and TV people, random celebrities—without me in them. What did they do—run back into the room with a camera after I split?

She didn't want my ex-bandmates. She wanted me.

BUT I HATE HOW
I LOOK IN PICTURES

I was inconsistent with her imagined version of me. "You must be into motorcycles, right?" I'd never been on one. She was crestfallen.

The calls got weirder. She was talking about how her mother liked her sister better; how she'd sought out women to watch her ex-husband fuck; how that filled her with disorienting rage as it wildly aroused her. Then she said she wanted to sleep with me.

My initial demurral was: But I don't know what you look like.

"But I can't send you a picture—I hate the way I look in pictures," she said.

I kept taking her calls. I thought that if I displeased her she'd nix me and go to my ex-bandmates, who would erase me.

HIPPEST SIDES

I told her that my favorite best-of title was *Bo Diddley's Hippest Sides*.

"Soul Coughing's Hippest Sides!"

There's a kitschy-beatnik connection people make with Soul Coughing; I'm not crazy about it.

"But it's a great title," she said. *"Soul Coughing's Hippest Sides."*

That's not how I want the songs framed.

I got a FedEx: cover mock-ups for *Soul Coughing's Hippest Sides*.

There was also a Polaroid with her face blurred out.

I was dreading her calls. I got migraines.

All record companies are manipulative. The most pressure I've ever experienced came from this person at this groovy reissue company.

She always deflected my assertions with *but I'm an artist, too.*

"Which did you like best?"

These are my songs. I don't want them contextualized like that.

Long pause. I could hear rage snowballing.

"They're *my songs, too!*" she snapped.

I went into a fugue state: trembling.

I said—weakly—that this was really unprofessional.

She gasped, deeply offended.

Professional? But *she's an artist, too.*

What I wish I said is: *Get the fuck away from my art. If you want to be an artist, make art.*

I got a FedEx of a new mock-up. The back cover was a band picture: the bar code had been put over my face.

OKAY OKAY OKAY OKAY OKAY OKAY OKAY OKAY OKAY OKAY OKAY

Now the album was finished and she contacted my ex-bandmates.

They were enraged by the liner notes. The rule was: don't talk about songwriting, because every single song had been improvised by the entire band all at once.

In a fury, the sampler player called her: she'd told him that, because the layout was done, sure, I could rewrite the entire liner notes—as long as it was precisely the same word count.

Somehow, he didn't absorb that she was blowing him off with sarcasm, and was now calling to ask me just that—and make sure it's exactly the same word count.

I asked him what he specifically wanted cut.

He said I should rewrite it.

I'd be very happy to make specific edits.

No, rewrite the whole thing.

Really, if there's stuff you don't like, it can be deleted, no problem.

But it would be better to rewrite it?

Two days later, he called the label again.

She called me up and verbally went through the deletions he asked for: Why didn't she email them?

I said yes to every deletion: okay, okay, okay, okay, okay, okay, okay, okay, okay, okay, okay.

SEE YOU

I was the musical guest on *The 24 Hour Plays* in Los Angeles.
I flew from St. Louis on show day; planned to fly to Chicago very
early on the day after—I was playing the Double Door that night.
How fiercely I love *The 24 Hour Plays*.

They put me up at a luxe hotel on Sunset. Sam Sifton, married
to the producer Tina Fallon, had come out to watch their daughter
while Tina worked.

Sam said, "I asked the concierge for help finding a breast pump.
He could probably find three hits of MDMA, a dominatrix, and a
forest-green 1967 MG convertible at three in the morning—but not
a breast pump."

I walked into my room to the sound of the phone ringing. I let
it go to voicemail. The red message light flashed, *cldk* pause *cldk*
pause *cldk* pause *cldk*.

It was her.

The phone rang again—this time, no voicemail. Again ten minutes later. My cell rang: her office number. No voicemail. Then her
home number. No voicemail. Then an unfamiliar 310 number.

Six calls in half an hour.

I snapped open the clamshell. Didn't say hi.

I'm in the middle of something.

"I want to *see* you," she said, "I really just want to *see* you."

I'm in the middle of something.

"I just need to see you," she said.

163

I'M IN THE MIDDLE OF SOMETHING I'M IN THE MIDDLE OF SOMETHING I'M IN THE MIDDLE OF SOMETHING.

I crushed the phone shut.

I *was* in the middle of something: my life.

During the show, I looked fearfully into the audience, scared she'd be there.

I wouldn't have recognized her if she was.

She didn't come. I think.

LOT (1995)

Soul Coughing played at the New Daisy on Beale Street in Memphis. Beale Street! W. C. Handy wrote "Beale Street Blues" in 1915; Riley B. King—later B.B.—adopted the title Beale Street Blues Boy in 1946; Furry Lewis swept the street in the 1960s.

Beale was in better shape than it was when Jim Jarmusch shot *Mystery Train* there in 1988: the city had begun transforming it into Bourbon Street Junior. Bands of polo-shirted middle-aged men roamed, clutching huge beers.

I walked up to a random old man and asked him where Stax had been.

"926 East McLemore," he said flatly—without hesitation.

Everyone who'd been in Memphis in the 1960s knew the address.

The building was razed in 1989. There were remnants of a floor. I wondered if I stood where Otis Redding had sung the word *mine* in 1962.

FADER (2004)

I opened for Galactic at the New Daisy. We wrote a song at sound check so I could come out and sing something with them. It was called "People Are Bad," and it went: *People are bad! Ship them back to personnel!*

Stax had been rebuilt as a museum: I woke up early the next day and went just as they were opening: I was alone in the exhibits. It starts in a theater, with a video compilation of Stax greats—a primer for people who came to Memphis for Elvis stuff.

I sat by myself, weeping at clips of Otis and Eddie Floyd.

Isaac Hayes's gold-and-teal Cadillac—fur-trimmed interior and a TV in the dashboard—is on a rotating platform. The most moving exhibit to me was Booker T. and the MGs' road cases: on them, in faded marker, was written the sound engineer's immortal admonishment: *Do Not Put Drinks Here*.

In the control room of the replica studio—looking around to make sure I was alone—I reached over the mixing board and pushed a fader.

INTEGRITY (1997)

The original Stax had a record store in front, built out of a refreshment stand. They weren't just selling Stax releases; it was for stealth research—watching sales, spinning rough mixes.

Estelle Axton—the Ax in Stax—monitored what kids were buying, then went to the writing and producing staff and reported what other labels were putting out: beats, topics, styles. The songwriting staff took the research and went to the pianos.

In 1997, a radio guy in Florida—complaining about all the dolorous grunge ballads—asked me if I'd consider writing an up-tempo song. Everyone in earshot thought it was a shocking violation.

SIDE ONE OF
LED ZEPPELIN IV (1982)

Skip Gill's sister Becky put on *Led Zeppelin IV* as we drove back from Great Adventure in her boyfriend's car. "The Battle of Evermore" came on as we were passing the oil refinery in Jersey—a cluster of towers dotted with yellow lights. Like a magic city choked with the smell of petroleum.

The spidery guitars and the keening; the lyrics foretold Satanic catastrophe. Later, Skip Gill and I would sit with a cassette player, riveted, stopping and rewinding, transcribing the lyrics. Looking to break the code.

The world was absolutely new.

When "Stairway" came on—the uncanny flute—I said, What is this?

"You really never heard this?" asked Becky's boyfriend, at the wheel.

He had just gotten a tattoo of a skull and the words ROCK RULES. Everyone seeing it for the first time asked in puzzlement, "*Rook* rules?"

I sought the knowledge. I'd go to the periodicals room at the USMA library to read smudgy copies of *Rolling Stone*. The stack of tattered copies looked like a Mardi Gras float left to fade in the sun. Near immaculate piles of the *Economist* and *Soviet Life*.

I scraped up some leads, but you really needed an older sibling to know.

I scrounged $5.98 to buy the cassette of *Led Zeppelin II*, because *Rolling Stone* said Led Zeppelin's "Whole Lotta Love" was the greatest heavy metal song of all time. I got the tape because the vinyl LP cost three bucks more.

There was a class divide between those flipping through the record bins and those at the wall of cassettes, which was always in the back. That's where I was. I scanned the tall columns, knowing that there was some tape—among hundreds—as life-transforming as *Led Zeppelin IV.*

People talk about how great it was back when you bought records based on the cover. But most of the time you whiffed. There were wondrous surprises, but what made them sweet was rolling the dice and at last buying one that wasn't terrible.

I picked the wrong one. It lacked the demonic allure of *Led Zeppelin IV.* Two minutes into the first song, there's a boring stretch of thunder noises and moaning that goes on forever before the guitar solo.

It was through Led Zeppelin that I learned not all records are the same just because it's the same band.

Maybe I should've known this by side two of *Led Zeppelin IV.* *Couldn't they have done something exactly like side one, but different?*

But I had skin in the game now: I listened to *Led Zeppelin II,* on my Walkman, over and over again, on car trips to the house my dad bought in Lackawaxen, Pennsylvania, where mostly I watched a single, snowy UHF channel and was made to split logs. I was told that when it got cold I'd be glad I'd split those logs.

The tape slowed when the batteries ran low—Robert Plant as a lugubrious cow. I could click the Walkman off, wait ten seconds, then restart; the music would be normal for another minute.

I got more money and rolled the dice again, thinking I'd land one: *Houses of the Holy.* Despite the cover—naked girls crawling on a temple—it was worse. "The Rain Song," with the string section, sounded like WHUD—the easy-listening station playing constantly in my dad's orange Volkswagen Rabbit. WHUD's go-to was Johnny Mathis.

At last I got sensible: I bought *Led Zeppelin IV.* I mustered $8.98 and got the LP.

I didn't have a turntable, but my parents did: my dad listened to a Willie Nelson live album on it once, and then I think the stereo was never used again.

I never listened to my LP of *Led Zeppelin IV*. Was the stereo too directly in the traffic of my parents' glacial marriage? Too close to my dad drinking beer and brooding?

I would take *Led Zeppelin IV* from the albums in the cabinet—the Joan Baez albums my mom bought in college, four volumes of *Firestone Presents Your Favorite Christmas Carols*—and rotate it dejectedly in my hands.

WATERS (1997)

I was at Wigstock, on Labor Day, on the West Side piers by the Hudson River: the storied realm of hookups and poppers.

I stood next to a guy dancing in white briefs, with blue paint splashed arbitrarily on his torso. A short guy, blond pageboy cut, muscled and plucked.

Todd Terry's "Something Goin' On" was spinning.

Let it show! Feels good!

I didn't go to gay clubs because I'd be an outsider—especially in the drag world, where I thought the insults were real and I'd be eviscerated. Every Labor Day at Wigstock I could float into the crowd and not be called out for lack of credentials.

I loved this kind of diva house. Most of my friends couldn't stand the ceaseless beat and repetitive lyrics—which I think were aimed at the hearts of boys who grew up feeling malformed. Now in the city, now themselves, divas exhorting them explicitly: feel it, everybody, dance, let go, you and me, it's going to be all right.

"Something Goin' On" was breaking my heart.

Let your waters overflow! I want to see you dance!

The world was absolutely new.

COMPLEMENT (1990)

This looming Greek guy from Bay Ridge, Brooklyn, corralled the arty kids for an independent study of the *Odyssey*—for credit! It would culminate in a collaborative show.

Our school's ace squad of actor kids and writer kids: funny and stoned. I joined not because of the *Odyssey*, which, in the end, is about family—I was a teenager, I didn't want to think about family—but because I wanted to be a part of them.

We drank coffee, then we smoked weed, then we drank beer, then we drank liquor, talking about the unifying piece. I'd get a notebook.

I'll write dialogue? You do sketches?

They laughed. There was so much more discussion to be had!

After a few weeks, I stormed out, saying, I'm writing a play.

It was scandalous that I split from the pack; after that, they sneeringly excluded me.

At the semester's end I turned in, essentially, *The Resistible Rise of Arturo Ui*, but with fake-Mamet dialogue. Those guys didn't turn in anything—anything.

I've been a working artist since age twenty-three. What happened to those other guys? Varying forms of inactivity, until Facebook was invented, at which point the Greek guy started posting embeds of Kenneth Anger movies.

"We rolled our eyes at you, Doughty," said one of them, over dinner, twenty years later. "But you were the one that did it."

PISTOL (1989)

All the young guys in my playwriting classes wrote the same play over and over again: the scenario Beckett, the characters Jarmusch, the dialogue Mamet. Arch references to 1970s pop culture, like, *How crazy is it that hard-boiled detectives talk about Poco?* Endless rat-a-tat dialogue, scene after scene after scene of tedious, feisty dialogue. All ended the same way: one guy suddenly has a pistol and—twist—the other guy takes it from him and shoots him.

VISITATION (1975)

I had nightmares about angels as a child. I'd open a door or turn a corner, and there would be an angel radiating golden beams like spears. Screaming dissonant string music. I was rooted to the spot in terror, unable to lift my feet.

WORLD OF BREAD (1991)

When I was driving the ice-cream van, I lived in a shoddy building on Spring and Elizabeth. I slept in an interior room that had a window to the living room: an actual house window, panes and frame. It's how they built tenements in the nineteenth century. Multiple families were crammed into apartments—it was ventilation.

This was years before they started calling the neighborhood Nolita. We called it Laundrytown, because unoccupied stores— almost all were unoccupied—had in their windows stacks of what looked like stuffed laundry bags.

The summer before I'd moved in, street scenes for *The Godfather Part III* had been shot on Elizabeth Street. They didn't bother to take down the fake signs—tailor, butcher, locksmith. I'd need a hammer or a key or something and find that behind the hardware store sign were just stacks of bags. Every empty store: stacks of mysterious bags.

Other neighborhood features:

A drug-front bodega on Spring. I don't know what in particular they sold, but I went in to buy cigarettes and found that their deli case held only a severed pig's head.

The Ravenite Social Club, the headquarters for John Gotti's crew. People said that when they met, you could tell by the smell of all the cologne.

The Shark Lounge. In the window I often saw my upstairs neighbor, a little person with a mullet. He had a permanently aggressive expression, like he was about to punch somebody. I came home once to find him lugging a massive subway route sign up the stairs.

Ray's Pizza, on Prince Street, which I was astonished to learn—in 2011, when it closed—was the *actual* original Ray's. I'd be getting a pesto-and-ricotta slice, and the counter dudes would be talking to an old guy named Ray. "I saw *the actual Ray!*" I joked with friends.

It turned out this was *actually for real the actual Ray.*

A store called Just Shades. No lamps: literally just shades. It was the setting for a classic Letterman remote, where he asked them repeatedly for things that weren't shades: "Do you have bulbs? Do you have extension cords?"

A maker of gravestones, who had a sort of sculpture garden behind a chain-link fence. You know, for junkies who'd steal giant hunks of granite.

A bread factory on the corner of Prince and Elizabeth. We came home from clubs at 4 a.m., walking off the acid, and the whole deserted world smelled like bread.

FLYERS

I'd walk home from the ice-cream place and see a flyer guy on Broadway improvising a song:

Come inside! There's a flea market inside!
Come inside to the flea market!
Flea market, there's a flea market!
Come inside to the flea market inside!

He did variations, but he was working long days, so it settled into a numb melody.

Excruciating.

He had a way of snapping the paper to get people to take flyers. I'd promise myself, *I'm not taking the flyer, I'm not taking the flyer, I'm not taking the flyer.*

Then *snap!* and some impulse to reach for snapping things made me take it.

I walked away enraged. Every time.

I saw a local-color piece in the *Villager* about him; he was a magnet for tourists with camcorders.

"I think I must be extremely famous in Europe," he said.

A CHANGE (1983)

On a cold night, we were driving away from the Nanuet Mall in my mom's beige Accord. The battery in my Walkman was low; stop-wait-start bought five seconds at most.

In despair I switched to radio.

It was nihilism: there'd be nothing there. Some periodic Led Zeppelin on WPDH? Please. Half that music had saxophones. Like you'd hear Judas Priest.

"King of Pain" was on. I heard the two-note bass figure and the tick-tock kalimba.

In spite of my principles I was transfixed.

Then the Eurythmics, "Here Comes the Rain Again," synths cascading from its heart.

The ice on the car was white; the light shining on the emptying parking lot was white; the salted road was white.

The world was absolutely new.

The next day I remembered myself and returned to heavy metal. But I could see that time would come. I dreaded it.

CONTROL (2011)

I matched on Tinder with a beautiful woman: I assumed she was fake, so I wrote something flattering but open-ended. Her responses seemed human.

Is there a Turing test for catfish? Did she pass or fail? Or did I? How does the Turing test work?

We met on MacDougal Street—one of the preserved beatnik places from what an older friend of mine called *the folk scare*—near where she was going to nursing school. She was reading a biology textbook when I walked in.

Her lips were oddly plump and her nose oddly slender. Surgery? There was something weirdly perfect about how centered her nose ring was on her nostril.

I found an innocuous way to ask why she was becoming a nurse at this point in her life; she found an innocuous way to say she was rich and staying busy. Her father was a movie producer in his eighties. She was the final daughter from his sequence of marriages.

She was fascinated that I was a musician. Knew nothing about it. Many questions—like a sociologist studying a Sardinian gleaner.

The previous weekend she'd taken a helicopter to her father's estate in the Hamptons. She said she didn't want to spend the weekend in traffic. She sounded like I did when embarrassed I could afford taxis to Astoria.

She was looking for an apartment: she teased her father that she'd leave Manhattan, and he'd said, "No daughter of mine will live in Brooklyn!"

He was buying her a condo in a blue-glass tower near the High Line.

We went to a Vietnamese place in Williamsburg for the next date. Lemongrass by candlelight. She told me about her piercings—most not visible.

I asked whether she wanted to walk on the bridge. "Is it safe?" she asked.

Yes, I said. It's no longer 1985.

We came to the bridge's midpoint; looked at the lights of the Baruch Houses, felt the brackish breeze. I thought that I was supposed to kiss her and that she wanted me to kiss her.

"I was worried you weren't going to," she said. "At dinner, you never looked at my tits."

I was touching her back. When my hands went to her sides, then up, they were stopped by a band of elasticized fabric. She said she chose the blouse because she wanted me to touch her in a controlled sequence: touch x at n time, touch y at r time. Message: horny, organized.

It's ungentlemanly to google a woman until after the third date—but I did, right when I got home. I found a photo of her at one of my shows.

I didn't need contextual clues—it said *Mike Doughty show at City Winery.*

I wrote a politely bewildered email.

She emailed back: she'd forgotten, she'd gone with a friend, how funny.

What if I pretended I hadn't seen it? Fast-forward ten years: I'm married to the horny, organized woman; I've accepted her control, submitted to her money; I'm spending my life in her blue tower, making my weird music.

ANGLE (1994)

There was a small pool of photographers who took pictures of bands, and there was ludicrous cash in music. Some were fabulous artists; others had just learned to put the lens above chin lines. *Stick your head a little forward, okay?*

Everybody has this skill set now—selfie angles. We see the tricks: *Oh, please.*

But it was big money: *This guy's a magician! The band looks incredible!*

SNARE (1989)

J. Why? needed a snare drum, so we went to the music stores on West Forty-Eighth Street. They'd served session players working at RCA on Sixth Avenue: radio in the '30s and '40s, TV in the '50s. At Manny's, all the wall space was framed photos—eye level were rock stars, high up were trumpeters and swing drummers. Studio orchestra guys, Broadway pit-band guys.

We Buy Guitars was a single counter. A line of dudes would be trying to sell their guitars: an elderly man appraised them grimly, barking lowball offers—weakly protested then accepted. In their window was a B.C. Rich Warlock—a 1980s-metal guitar shaped like a pointy spider—painted as a *Pac-Man* screen. The ghosts, the cherries, the maze.

A guy came up to us. "You looking to buy drums?" We walked past him.

"You want the LL33? I got the Yunex 47, I got the Shine Crabber ..."

J. Why? stopped. He said a brand.

The guy nodded like, *Of course, what, are you stupid?*

J. Why? asked him if he was telling the truth.

"Like I'm trying to *steal* from you?"

What if we give you half the money and the other half when you bring it?

"Okay. I don't know if that'll fly. Okay. I'll ask him. Don't follow me, he won't like that. He won't give me the deal."

He walked around the corner; ten suspenseful minutes passed.

He came back shaking his head.

"He doesn't like it. No. But good news. Okay. He'll do ten bucks even cheaper on the Shine Crabber."

J. Why? had to have it.

In the suburbs, we were told how perilous Manhattan was. There was a public service campaign: *Don't flash your cash!* He counted the bills close to his chest and palmed it to the guy.

The guy said, "Don't move, don't go into Rudy's, stay here."

We nodded. J. Why? was overjoyed. "Don't go anyplace. This doorway. Right here."

Yes, we understand, yes.

By the time we knew he'd stolen the money, we'd put in too much time to leave. We were Didi and Gogo. An hour and a half passed.

We went to a diner. I was broke. J. Why? bought me a cheeseburger.

ADDENDUM ON *PAC-MAN* (1982)

In the original Japanese, the *Pac-Man* monsters were Fickle, Chaser, Ambusher, and Stupid.

When I was twelve, the Middletown *Times Herald-Record* quoted a doctor who warned that tender psyches won't recover from *Pac-Man*'s metaphors: running through tunnels, devouring, never satisfied, pursued by monsters.

There was a rumor that unscrupulous arcades gave out credit: play all the *Pac-Man* you want, get a bill in January. Families penniless, homes lost.

ZIGGURAT (1997)

Soul Coughing played New Orleans on Halloween. Not a packed show. Hard to blame the people of New Orleans—if I'd lived there, I'd be into trombone players and uninterested in alternative rock.

Though I've heard New Orleans has an exceptional death-metal scene.

A sexy fat woman came up to me. "It's good to see you!" I didn't know who she was.

She talked about how she had been doing merch for classic-rock bands since I'd last seen her in Wisconsin. She brought me an armload of Deep Purple and Styx shirts.

"I don't know what your size is, so I got you XLs," she said.

She said she had a bunch of mushrooms, did I want to come back to her hotel?

We went.

We chewed the particleboard-consistency mushrooms in her room, which had a courtyard. Deep Purple treated their crew well.

She had a piece of paper—Xerox of a Xerox—with a diagram of a hotel cable box and a bullet-pointed sequence for pushing the remote buttons: how to get free pay-per-view. A sacred document passed between bands' crews.

I began to feel that sizzle—the trip coming on.

Cut to: we're fucking in her courtyard.

I started to think I was going to orgasm too fast, so I slowed down, but she moved her hips and ground against me faster.

"Go ahead," she said. "We're going to do it again and again. Again and again."

I did not want to do it again and again.

I came; the atmosphere wobbled.

I tried to cook up an excuse, but my brain was also wobbling. I think I said nonsense syllables and walked out. I felt like a guy in an earthquake movie trying to get under a desk. I had to get out before I was fully tripping. The portal was closing!

"Don't you want to fuck in the City of the Dead?" she called after me, outraged.

I got a cab. The driver was a Sikh guy who seemed very, very angry at me. We drove down Esplanade; people walking under the iron balconies seemed like werewolves out to gnaw throats.

We were staying at a Days Inn by the airport.

I got into the room and decided that I could sleep.

It wasn't until the early 2000s that hotel chains realized they could charge fifty bucks extra if they had monochrome bedspreads. The Days Inn's bedspread was floral upheaval. It, too, seemed to be very angry.

I closed my eyes and saw a mountain-sized machine. I was standing miles away from it—it was like viewing Mount Rainier from Seattle on a clear day. But the sky wasn't blue; it was yellow—a busy yellow, like a wall in a Vermeer painting. Brushed not with light, but with dirt.

I was flying. I floated closer to the mountain-machine.

It was made of clarinets and steam engines. Smokestacks with trumpet valves expelled puffs. Each puff was a cloud of wild music. There was an ominous, atonal *thrmmmmmmmm* that the machine-mountain made, dotted with sharp pops of trumpet and clarinet.

Windows snapped open: there would be a painting of a guy in a World War I naval uniform, or an American flag—a cocktail-sausage flag on a toothpick—would shoot out and wave spastically.

I was like the guy in *The Greatest American Hero* who couldn't control the superhero suit. I tried to fly up and instead went down; I tried to bank right and instead zoomed toward the peak.

I realized that this was the divine ziggurat of New Orleans, which existed beyond time and before the existence of New Orleans. I also realized that it was very small, and I was also very, very small.

I opened my eyes and went to the hotel room's beige telephone. There was a light blinking on it, which, if I listened closely— I couldn't not listen closely—made a little sound like *cldk* pause *cldk* pause *cldk* pause *cldk*.

I checked the voicemail. I had a message from this extremely normal girl in South Carolina. I was funny-looking, talked weirdly, and made references to *All About Eve*. I didn't do well with normal girls until I was kind of famous.

"Thanks for your message," she said in her small voice. "It was rad."

ADDENDUM ON
SEXY FAT WOMAN (2005)

I played a bar in Iowa and was surprised to find the sexy fat woman managing it. Neither she nor I acknowledged the hallucinogens, sex, and abandonment in New Orleans.

She came into the dressing room before I went on, told me she felt sick and definitely there wouldn't be anybody else coming to the show who wasn't in the bar already and she was leaving so she had to pay me now and by the way she had to pay me in cash, okay?

It wasn't big money, but the rubber-banded tens and twenties—bar cash—was bulky. She was gone by the time I realized that on-stage my pockets would bulge absurdly with rolls of cash.

FAMOUS (2006)

I was in a Rhode Island mall; a woman burst into tears and hugged me. It was like being clotheslined.

The rest of the mall was bewildered.

"I saw your show last night, those songs are *just so beautiful*," she said.

I autographed something for a dude at a storage facility on Second Avenue. I was getting an amp out of my space; he was astonished to run into me.

A lady in a huge puffy coat walked up, said "Are you famous?," and then demanded a picture.

STAIRS (1988)

My film-history class watched *Battleship Potemkin*, the 1925 silent film—the famous sequence where a lady gets shot in the eye and a baby carriage rolls toward the Cossacks. Then we read an essay by Sergei Eisenstein decrying continuity as bourgeois. Everybody loved that.

I skipped a showing of *Vertigo* one week, for the same reason I skipped more conventionally-difficult classes: I was paralyzed by depression. I thought it was sloth.

I went to the teacher, embarrassed, asking to borrow the VHS tape to watch in the library.

"Don't feel bad," she said. "Nobody plays hooky on watching a movie."

I couldn't watch the movie because I had to share the VHS room with a guy breaking down a shipment of mushrooms into Ziploc bags. He was a French-Canadian hippie guy, seen by all as sunny and beatific. He played Bach partitas on guitar at the talent show.

In the VHS room, he was a scowling paranoiac. I was unable to watch Jimmy Stewart in the glow of his chaos.

Wracked with self-hate for my sloth, I didn't watch *His Girl Friday* either, or *Five Easy Pieces*, or *La Nuit Américaine*. On down through the semester.

SING COLA (1986)

J. Why? was a fastidious roommate; I wasn't. Particularly with records. I left his copy of *King of America* on the turntable.

On "Brilliant Mistake," Elvis Costello sings the words *Coca-Cola* more achingly than anyone has ever sung a brand name.

The world was absolutely new.

The vinyl got dusty and J. Why? was furious.

I took a toy duck his girlfriend gave him and stuck it in the Shenandoah's Pride milk crate holding his albums. He threw it at me violently.

It was soft, so it could only fall gently to the rug.

He hated cigarettes—hated any drug. I wanted to learn how to smoke. I got a pack of Marlboro Lights and stood at the mirror, watching myself smoke the whole pack. I couldn't have inhaled, because I didn't get sick. It was unclear where the cigarette ended and the filter began; the room smelled like burnt spork.

Each room had a nonoperational fire detector called *the cosmic nipple*. Our room looked like a Mötley Crüe video.

HIPPO MUNGO DAZZY DOLF

J. Why? tried out for the basketball team, and I asked, How was the audition?

He had a book of vintage baseball statistics, which I loved for the names:

Urban Shocker
Noodle Hahn
Orville Overall
Rube Marquard
Hippo Vaughn
Burleigh Grimes
Dazzy Vance
Dolf Luque
Preacher Roe
Van Mungo
Chief Bender
Flint Rhem
Firpo Marberry
Jumbo Elliott

ME AND MY (2017)

I was DMing with a woman who'd been the love interest in a classic stoner movie. While we walked into a restaurant, skater kids across the street yelled her character's name.

Her other signature role was in a teen-goth classic, which made her an improbable goth icon. She was writing a book on a witchy topic—very on brand—and wanted to go to New Orleans. Did I want to meet her there?

I drove down from Memphis.

Goth-y places in the French Quarter welcomed her as royalty. She was invited to a hidden witch bar—there was a password, and the door was *locked behind us*—where a shitfaced witch explained how to build an altar, and how it's important to keep salt on hand to repel the surly dead.

The actor and I weren't getting along, but we'd made a flirty deal: I'd pay for the hotel, she'd buy me a psychic reading. It became our grim date-pact.

I asked the drunk witch who to see; he said he got his readings from a priestess that nobody liked because she was so cryptic. His quotes of her sounded like John Ashbery poems.

"I can recommend you somebody you'd be more into," said the drunk witch.

No, I think this is *exactly* the priestess I want to see.

Her door was locked when we went. It was not a good day. The actor and I had done the entire arc of a bad relationship in thirty-six hours. On the priestess's doorstep, we barked at each other about who botched the VIP tour of the City of the Dead.

The door slowly opened.

The priestess spoke as if through a tube from the other world—disconnected, like a schizophrenic's speech, but also like a slowed-down Emily Dickinson, the words jumping on hyphens around the page. Or a Cocteau Twins song, where you can barely make out lyrics through the reverb.

We stood in the shop for an hour as she shuffled around, speaking elliptically, arranging candles. Then she looked at me in puzzlement and said, "You came here for a reading, didn't you?"

She indicated the reading room's door, then turned and pointed at the actor.

"You answer the phone," she said. To a movie star!

The reading room was filled with statues of saints and creatures, each piled with offerings: coins, cigarettes, rosaries, playing cards, mini bottles of liquor, Bic lighters. She took out a bag of bones and shells and tossed them on the table like she was shooting dice.

The phone rang relentlessly in the next room. The actor answered it in the style of a sitcom receptionist. She couldn't get a word in edgewise; the callers were panicked, they needed to talk to the priestess, is this the priestess, where's the priestess?

The actor responded in a Californian language of centering and energy. She was sincerely trying to help, but she couldn't stop herself from making it about herself. Her voice was very loud.

"What is she trying to do?" said the priestess, bewildered.

I got out my phone, placed it on the table between us, and recorded the reading into GarageBand. It was ninety minutes long. It was sometimes hard to follow, veering into opinions about gun control and property taxes. But she'd return to them twenty minutes later and connect them, like a comic doing callbacks. Random things resolved into haunting metaphors.

An hour in, she stopped.

"So you have *questions*?" said the priestess, in a tone like, *What's up with you?*

I asked her for a poem.

"Oh ho ho ho ho," said the priestess. "That's funny." She raised her head and recited: "*Me and my beautiful Annabel Lee, in a sepulchre by the sea.*"

Edgar Allan Poe—imprecisely—from a voodoo priestess, in a room of statues, dolls, candles, baskets, flags, paintings, nails, swords.

The world was absolutely new.

She just said those two lines. I wondered if it was a blow-off—this goofball is asking for *poetry*? She went back into the half-comprehensible monologue.

Fifteen minutes later, she landed the metaphor: "So you see, *that* is your Annabel Lee, and he is *her* sepulchre, and you, *your* sepulchre is what you're doing to *yourself*, because your Annabel Lee is . . ."

It was an incredible performance—I don't mean that to say it was fake, though I don't think I believe in a hidden sphere into which gifted souls can see. I heard it as a long poem, with line breaks and measured rhythms.

I drove back to Memphis. On I-55, it came into my head again, as it keeps coming into my head: *Me and my beautiful Annabel Lee, in a sepulchre by the sea.*

GEMINI (1990)

I got my heart broken at the end of a school year; she left me for my drummer. Yet she'd picked *me* up: her line was, "You've got a body like Jesus."

I spent the boiling summer in shock: How could I feel this bottomless feeling?

I read *NYPress* every week—I got it from a steel box in front of the Puck Building. It was a golden period for them. In the back, among the classifieds, were the classic comic strips by Kaz, Mark Beyer, Carol Lay, Takeshi Tadatsu, the little-remembered, genius strip by David Lynch, *The Angriest Dog in the World.* Also back there was Rob Brezsny's *Real Astrology.*

I read Gemini and Aquarius every week, desperate to hear that the girl who broke my heart was lonely, and that I was destined to get her back.

When the desperation was gone, my faith in astrology was gone, too. But that guy is a great writer—and he had a band with an amazing name: World Entertainment War.

Some weeks, inexplicably, it wouldn't be there. I would sit on a peeling bench in Tompkins Square flipping through, then re-flipping, in boggled distress.

When, years later, I worked for *NYPress*, John Strausbaugh told me they didn't run the column sometimes, just because they were amused by the anguished pleading of its fans. I think, though, that they—eventually, we—resented how so many people picked up the paper just for the astrology.

The *Village Voice* eventually realized that *NYPress* was gaining on them—it was noisy and vengeful in a way they hadn't been for years—and so, among other things, they sent Rob Brezsny an overwhelming bid. *NYPress* declined to match it.

"Those guys are a dime a dozen," sneered the publisher.

They weren't.

CASHMERE DAN (2004)

I wanted to start working with a band again, but I didn't know anybody. I'd spent half the 1990s getting high and watching marathons of *The Real World*; I'd spent the 2000s touring alone. My professional network was tundra.

I put something on my blog.

I met some drummers, one of whom was a guy from Scranton named Gene—not the right drummer, but I wanted to hire him just so I could introduce him onstage by the nickname Pennsylvania Gene. I got an email from him recently: he became a Navy SEAL.

Another drummer's audition was fantastic so I hired him, but at each successive rehearsal he played worse—and worse, and still worse. It was a feat.

What a weird conversation to avoid having with a drummer as you're firing him.

I met the piano player Dan Chen at his studio, beneath a derelict bodega. I'd sent four songs to everybody but discovered that I knew if I liked them in the first thirty seconds—I'd given pointless homework.

I immediately knew Dan was the guy. He did that grimy bells sound. He dug into the chords, put ornaments in nice spots, took the light when the vocal ceded it.

Dan got the job, the audition was over, but I felt obligated to run through the tunes; on the third song, he flubbed the bridge and the tune collapsed.

"Can we do that again from the top?"

Oh, that's all right—we don't have to—I should get out of here.

It was weird that the first musician auditioned would be the guy, but he was the guy.

But to Dan, it looked like the audition fell apart at the first fuckup.

I was so cheerful as I left, which must've been off-putting, but I couldn't say, I just have to go through the formality of auditioning ten people I made learn four songs.

He was shocked when I called to hire him.

QUIK (2011)

There's a coffee roaster I like; I go there and pretend to understand what they're talking about. Then I buy the second-most-expensive beans. Because a dilettante would buy the *most* expensive beans.

They're kept in jars. The roaster unscrews the caps, carefully swirls the beans around. You lower your face to the jar and sniff.

"This has overtones of pinewood and yarn." I sniffed.

"This has notes of asphalt and dead leaves." I sniffed.

"This one smells like Strawberry Quik." *It really smelled like Strawberry Quik.*

I bought a half pound for thirty bucks.

I BELONG (1974)

I rolled around the back seat of a gargantuan Oldsmobile—a
small, fat child on an immense expanse of forest-green vinyl—
listening to *John Denver's Greatest Hits* on a shoebox-sized tape
recorder. I rewound, replayed, rewound, replayed "Take Me Home,
Country Roads."

The world was absolutely new.

NEGATIONS (1999)

I got an email from a woman who'd been in a band with somebody I knew. They'd been on a label but didn't put out a record. I gave her my number: she sang a slurry "Janine" on my voicemail but sounded weirdly not-drunk.

We met at the Odessa of Light, down Avenue A from the Odessa of Darkness. The former served disco fries; the latter was a drink-yourself-to-death cave.

She had good jokes about psych meds. I told her I wished I had better jokes about mine.

She said that when her dependency on them irritated her she'd throw them out.

She said her band had been great, but the label betrayed them.

She told me her parents were the co-popes of a famous cult.

She'd gone to the same school as me.

She wouldn't stop talking about how she had no chance as an artist, that there was no hope, that it was over.

Why think that way, if—

"No, no, I'm too old, there's no way."

You could—

"You don't understand, it's over, it's not going to happen for me!"

How violating to be pulled in, then punched in the face.

I listened to the blue-back CD-R she gave me. I was floored: these anguished songs climbing deliberately up the melodic register; higher on every verse; her voice breaking, howling.

The world was absolutely new.

I called and said I loved it.

She said I was wrong, and it was the very worst.

Maybe I should've said, *You're right, it's bad, you're old.*

Instead I stopped calling.

She emailed me and said she loved me.

She kept emailing me, every day, saying she loved me. It was more violating than the negation of praise.

I wrote—how did I find these words?—to her, *You don't have that kind of access.*

Now she was leaving voicemails, longer and longer, tearful: I was stealing from her. I'd kidnapped her brother.

She stopped calling. Or did she? I got rid of my landline.

NEGATIONS (2006)

She showed up at a show in Hoboken before sound check and gave me a gift: a small purple box. I know that gifts are often how a stalker gets in the door—it creates an obligation. But I took it. I left it on my amp.

I came back to the stage to play the show and the purple box was gone. I asked my band if they'd seen the box; asked the bartender and the sound person if they'd seen someone onstage.

I didn't see her in the audience or after the show.

NEGATIONS (2014)

I opened Instagram and found comments on a hundred posts: *I still love you—I'll always love you—I'll never stop loving you.*

Working her way back years in my feed. What can be so exceptionally violating about *I love you*? Like shears gouging my face.

I didn't respond. My therapist says that the only effective thing to do with stalkers is: *be boring.*

NEGATIONS (2019)

I'm still listening to her incredible songs. They're on my pure-pleasure playlist, for long drives or for when I'm losing energy: twenty-two hours and eleven minutes of exhilaration.

Other songs in the playlist: the Clash, "Train in Vain"; Belle and Sebastian, "The Boy with the Arab Strap"; BDP, "My Philosophy"; Bowie, "John, I'm Only Dancing"; Ned's Atomic Dustbin, "Grey Cell Green"; Halo Benders, "Don't Touch My Bikini"; Rich Homie Quan, "Type of Way"; Black Sabbath, "The Wizard"; Prince, "Sign o' the Times"; Audio Two, "Top Billin'."

Does anyone else listen to her songs? They're demos—does someone who used to work at her label listen and feel the yearning what-ifs?

I got an email from my manager: "Do you know somebody named _____? They signed up for your Patreon. They've been systematically commenting on every single post going back two years."

I BELONG (1988)

We let everybody who didn't want bunk beds put the frames in our mod. No mattresses—just the steel frames. The living room looked like Thunderdome until my roommates hung tapestries on them.

I was on acid, lying on the floor. A hippie guy named Josh was in there, listening to *American Beauty* on a box.

I was in a creative writing class with him. Someone had written a story about Hasidim; he didn't know what that meant.

"What's a *hass-id*?" he'd asked.

He was watching me watch the ceiling fan.

"You're going to be frying for a while," he said, and left.

He came back with a circular bungee cord, about the height of a person, and put it in my hands. I twisted it around my arms, stretched it, was wholly absorbed.

He put on the Beatles. *A lucky man who made the grade.* The dumbfounding orchestral crescendo.

I didn't recognize the next album. Reggae? Very soulful.

"I belong," sang the reggae singer.

"You've never heard this?" said Josh.

It was Toots and the Maytals' version of "Take Me Home, Country Roads." Of course, it would've been childish to listen to John Denver—there was music I listened to in secret because it was uncool, but I don't think returning to John Denver ever occurred to me. Even as I was pulled into it, my thought was that Toots and the Maytals had somehow made this a good song, not that a John Denver song could be anything but unmentionable.

Something in my interior was touched.

The world was absolutely new.

"I go to bed—but sleep don't come," sang Toots, sounding overjoyed about it.

TOTO IS
THE TOTO OF THE '90S (1991)

J. Why? and a trombone player named Squantch were at the Berklee College of Music, riffing about who the Toto of the '90s was. A muscle-shirted shredder with a guitar in a gig bag stopped at their table

"Excuse me," he said. "Toto's still around. *Toto is the Toto of the '90s.*"

FREQUENCIES (2011)

I had two shows that summer: a daytime thing on the shore near Providence, and a daytime thing at a food festival in Chicago. Both well-paid.

The bookers for each wanted a full band, not my acoustic thing. When I get these inquiries, my agent calls and says, "Full band, okay?" and I say, Sure, easy. I worry about hiring a band later.

I had Scrap and I had a piano player: Cashmere Dan. I needed a drummer. Scrap knew a dude but spoke of him agnostically.

I auditioned him: he was good.

At rehearsal he got worse.

A bandleader tries to coax performances: stay cheerful, focus on their best playing. This guy got more nervous, more nervous, every time I said something; after a tune I'd smile diplomatically and tell him to maybe be more careful about the top of the second chorus?

He'd explode in anxiety, *HA HA HA HA HA.*

Eventually I was turning to him and saying, Look, you have to be better.

In Rhode Island he was a sweat amoeba.

He knew he wouldn't be playing with us again, which made it both easier and harder to be with him in the van as we drove back.

I had a week to hire somebody for Chicago. I asked everybody I knew and got thirty names. I only looked at drummers with You-Tube links, so I could watch them, not just hear them. The best drummer was a woman who'd played arenas with Beyoncé. She was beyond confident—appropriately—and clearly the loudest, funniest person on the tour bus. She wanted $5,000 for one show. I didn't chisel her.

"Okay, next time!" she said.

I had fifteen YouTube windows open. I wrote to each drummer. There wasn't time for auditions—I had to hire on the basis of the video.

I narrowed it down to four and picked a dude. One rehearsal tomorrow, then we fly to Chicago and play the show. He's in. Okay, great.

He had a Jewish-hobbit name, which I will simulate here as Frodo Lefkowitz. It was a funny name for a black dude.

The next morning, I was idling on Facebook; it occurred to me to add Frodo Lefkowitz as a friend. I looked him up and found a profile pic of a stout white dude with a mustache, in a guayabera shirt and big Cazal glasses.

That's weird, the Frodo Lefkowitz I'm looking for is a black guy with a shaved head. This must be a different Frodo Lefkowitz. How funny that there's multiple Frodo Lefkowitzes on Facebook.

Oh no.

I ran to the rehearsal studio, hoping I'd get there in time to tell Scrap and Cashmere Dan that I hired a guy I didn't mean to hire.

Frodo Lefkowitz was behind the kit when I walked in. Scrap and Cashmere Dan were plugging in. They were laughing—Frodo Lefkowitz was a joy. Clearly fun to be in a band with.

Then we started playing. Frodo Lefkowitz wasn't good.

Very subtly, Scrap and Cashmere Dan looked at me while we were running through the tunes. *This* is the guy?

We took a break. Frodo Lefkowitz expressed his pleasant surprise at getting a job as a drummer, being that he was a piano player.

By the time we got to Chicago, Frodo Lefkowitz knew the tunes, but he had beginner-drummer problems—hitting the snare at wildly varying velocities, slowing down, speeding up. Mostly, he was worried about needing too much time to catch his breath.

We worked out a thing based on the *Portlandia* sketch where Fred Armisen and Carrie Brownstein played a couple using *cacao!* as a safe word during sex. If he started feeling like he needed to pause, Frodo Lefkowitz could shout *cacao, cacao!* from behind the drum kit.

Of course, he took it as an issue of pride and endured the muscle fatigue. I really wanted there to be some yelling of *cacao!* during the set, but he didn't.

What a charming presence, though. Merry, and an entertaining teller of anecdotes. He must've known something was up, because he said I should drop him a line if Cashmere Dan were unavailable for something.

The festival's headliner was a classic alternative-rock band who had some big hits—of course, bigger than Soul Coughing. I'd always envied them, but the music was tedious to me.

Frodo Lefkowitz turned to me while they were playing.

"Aren't those frequencies just in the air *anyway*?" he said.

DERBY

That day, as we landed in Chicago, I got a *NYTimes* alert. Only part of the subject line was visible: *BREAKING: Singer Amy Wi . . .*

I texted a friend—a roller-derby person, lots of tattoos. She'd just gotten sober. How corny to be reminded by all the tattoos, but I was grateful she was alive.

Silence.

When she texted back, she said she'd realized she'd never had a weed problem and if she only drank beer maybe when she wasn't working and kept careful track of it? She'd be fine.

FISH-FACED MAN (1996)

Soul Coughing was being considered for the soundtrack of *The X-Files*. There were albums coming out all the time called *Music from and Inspired by the Original Motion Picture*, usually with only a song or two that were actually in the movie. People bought a ton of them.

I'd never seen *The X-Files*. My manager sent VHS tapes. I liked the one where the guy named Duane Berry keeps repeating, "Duane Berry, Duane Berry."

I told the producers I was a huge fan, just huge.

They gave us money.

I wrote a song called "Unmarked Helicopters," summarizing themes of millennial anxiety: abductions, cover-ups, mystical lights over dark suburbs. I drew on everything Gen X was told about UFOs on corny television in the 1970s.

We hit it out of the park. The song made it onto the actual show: Mulder walks into a mobile home where the song is blasting; he clicks the stereo off and removes a cassette tape on which *Soul Coughing* is written.

I went to a wrap party in Los Angeles at which Gillian Anderson was supposed to show up but didn't. I met Chris Carter, the guy who created the series.

"There's an episode coming out next week that I know you are going to love," he said.

I'm going to love it? It relates to my work? Have you read my poetry? But he was just speaking Hollywood and meant that it was a good episode.

The character actor Vincent Schiavelli was at this party. In the '80s and '90s, he was in everything. To name four: *Better Off Dead, Ghost, Buckaroo Banzai, Amadeus.*

When I was back in New York, I was excited to tell my friends that I saw the fish-faced man. I couldn't remember his name; this was long before Google.

"Which actor?"

You know, the fish-faced man!

"What was he in?"

He's—he was in everything!

"Like, what's one thing he was in?"

You know who I'm talking about, you totally know! The fish-faced man! The fish-faced man!

FROM AND INSPIRED BY (1997)

"Unmarked Helicopters," a list of talking points from Leonard Nimoy's 1977–1982 series *In Search Of*, was the lead single from the *X-Files* soundtrack. Fortune!

Chris Carter would direct the video when he was done shooting the season. But when he finished shooting, he said he was going on vacation for three months.

Who could begrudge him that? I could.

If we went with the plan, Warner Bros. would push back our album—*Irresistible Bliss*, on which the radio track was "Super Bon Bon"—for who knew how long? Months. What if the *X-Files* song got big? Years—and we were relying on money for shows after the album release.

Our manager at the time was useless when we needed motivating, and articulate when telling us how we fucked up. We needed to hear two things:

First: *If your problem is that you can't put out your own album because you have a giant hit single, that's an exceptionally luxurious luxury problem.*

Second: *Ask Warner Bros. for money to tide you over for those months, and they'll give it to you.*

Instead I lay awake in dread and resentment.

Every label in the 1990s had a rap about itself: people at Columbia pretended to be in the mafia; Geffen was gifted with magic power to monetize hipness; MCA stood for *music cemetery of America*, and, yeah, that's what they thought, too.

Warner Bros. saw itself as the defender of artistry. Prince, for instance, at age nineteen, said he didn't need a producer, and although any label might be sensible to tell a teenager they could use a producer, Warner Bros. trusted him—and made a ton of money.

Indulgence was bad for Soul Coughing. Artiest of artists though we were.

We were hell-bent on blowing opportunities. For instance, a video directed by the *X-Files* guy. I wish—I so desperately wish—that they'd forced us to do things we didn't want to do.

CONSIDER THE LONGBOX

The man whose job it was to talk us into it had a rap about himself, too: he was the man who killed the longbox.

The longbox was cardboard that held a CD case: a package to hold a package. It was the same length as an LP bin; it solved a stocking problem for record stores. Even when CDs outsold LPs, the longbox hung on.

He persuaded R.E.M. to put a postcard on their longbox, urging *[write congressperson's name here]* to support the Motor Voter Act of 1993—cut it out, stamp it, mail it to DC.

Then he concocted jiujitsu math: the record companies would pay for LP bins to be retrofitted, but the record stores were really paying for it, but actually the buyer paid for it; goodbye longbox, now everybody's making more money.

He was right to be proud of it—it was a feat.

He mentioned it whenever he spoke to any artist.

It was incomprehensible to us. *I solved a packaging problem!*

He got us on a conference call. He was at Warner Bros. headquarters: a building in Burbank that looked like a ski lodge; we were in a basement in Fort Greene.

He was persuasive: I was sold. I think the other guys were sold.

He didn't say Warner Bros. would give us money to live on. Our manager had to have mentioned that, right?

The drummer spoke up.

"Yo, G, why can't we release both albums on the same day?"

The longbox guy explained that retailers would be confused.

We were all persuaded, except:

"Yo, G, but why don't we just release both albums on the same day?"

The yo, G thing is real. I quoted him in my last book with a yo, G in maybe every third sentence, and literally I'd removed every other yo, G to make it believable.

The longbox guy did not say: *Warner Brothers spent money on you—and now we want to make money on you. You are a weird band, but maybe you'll be homeowners someday.*

"Yo, G, just put both the albums out on the same day."

Chris Carter didn't do the video; the soundtrack came out and pretty much died.

The precious heart of artistry had carried the day.

CROSS (2015)

Our tour bus was in a two-mile line of vehicles waiting to drive onto the ferry from Calais to Dover. It was four in the morning.

I was in the upstairs lounge—European tour buses are double-deckers—with the guitar player, trading a tiny practice guitar back and forth. We both were giddy because we loved the placelessness of tour life, how it was like living in a submarine—the bus had fourteen bunks, two lounges, a kitchenette.

We joked about being trapped in a steel box and drowning in the English Channel. His girlfriend was in the band and always insisted he obey the safety regulations, which require that you go up to the ferry's decks.

They never check. I like to stay asleep in my bunk. I trolled her by singing Celine Dion's "My Heart Will Go On."

We heard banging, then yelling. We ran to the window. Our bus driver and the merch seller were staring in disbelief past the equipment trailer.

There was a stage tech on the tour who did everything wrong: a sandy-haired kid from Liverpool, always smiling, unaware that he was fucking up. It was often something that crossed the implied line between band and crew. The band's paying the crew—the crew's working for the band—but to survive for two months in a land submarine, everybody pretends it's a collective.

This tech would pick up somebody's guitar—without asking—and shred; beatbox on somebody's mic during sound check. He got a cold, and though half the touring party had to sing every night, he sprawled in the upstairs lounge, hogging the banquette and the PlayStation, coughing, guzzling Fanta.

My friend Gus Brandt thinks that every tour should have somebody whose job is to be hated. *Who moved the amps? Jimmy? Jimmy—fucking Jimmy! Fuck that guy!*

So probably the kid forgot to latch the trailer, and drums and T-shirt boxes were strewn on the road. We ran outside.

The merch guy and the bus driver were staring angrily at a herd of unhitched trailers across the road. Staring something down.

The trailer was locked; nothing had fallen out of it. The bus driver, pointing: "They're right there. Still there."

Who?

The merch guy pointed. "You can see their feet. Look at them!"

Behind one of the trailers was a huddle of dudes. Their legs were visible. They looked like Shaggy and Scooby hiding behind a curtain.

"They fine you five thousand quid for each if they catch you smuggling them," said the bus driver.

Two dudes—refugees stuck in Calais, barred from the UK—had been running down the line of vehicles, tugging handles; they found the bus's luggage bay open and jumped in. The driver heard the door, ran out, yanked the dudes onto the road, and they ran.

The luggage bay was supposed to be locked.

"They can't be arrested. They'll do it again tomorrow," said the bus driver.

The whole bus was now awake—we were going to have to clear British passport control before the bus drove onto the ferry anyway—making nervous conversation in the kitchenette.

"I guess you really had to have an alibi," said the bass player to the guitar player.

"So what? I needed an alibi," said the guitar player.

"That alibi was really *super* necessary," said the bass player.

"What's wrong with that? Got to have my alibi," said the guitar player.

It was Cold War–torture-scene dark. I was so stressed out by it that I couldn't breathe, and I couldn't figure out a way to bolt without making a big deal of it.

But, in fact, an energy-drink company called Alibi had given them a case of their beverages, and the joke was that the guitar player had grabbed one from the luggage bay and left the door unlocked.

Naturally, the clueless guitar tech was the guy who didn't lock it. He sat with his hoodie pulled tight around his face during the alibi joke. His head in his hands.

Passport control had cattle gates to herd a snaking queue, like at Six Flags. But the only people in the harshly lit room were us, the customs agents, and the dudes who tried to stow away on our bus.

They were nervous. Drumming their hands. Their manner of dress was like casual Friday at a temp agency. One of them was singing under his breath.

I felt violated. I'd learned from a Jordanian teacher that eye contact is aggressive in Arab cultures, so I stared them directly in the eyes: *motherfuckers*.

A customs guy with a soft demeanor came up.

"So where are you guys from? Syria? Okay," he said, marking on a clipboard.

"They'll let them go," said the bus driver. "Could've been ten thousand quid!"

That was when I remembered things from TV: bombing, fleeing, white dust, blood, violent guards, gurneys, weeping, barriers, wire—and the Jungle, which is what they called the squalid refugee encampment in Calais.

SAD MAN EATS CANDY IN BED

I took Ambien for jet lag, and kept taking it when the jet lag was gone. I started doing that sleep-bingeing thing, killing boxes of cookies in a zombie state.

Okay, tonight, no eating, we'll just take this Ambien and be asleep, no eating.

Then I'm in the bus kitchenette throwing yogurt into my face, there but not there.

If you ever sleepwalk and are semi-aware while it's happening, you'll know this state: I became a half-self. I absolutely remember being that half-self and thinking, *To hell with you, waking-world person.*

I stopped keeping my phone in the bunk because I was sending apologies for ancient transgressions. I took the Ambien, promising myself I'd stay off the phone, then suddenly the half-self is sneering, *Ha! I'm on Facebook!*

I'd wake up in the bunk remembering the half-self typing something—seize the phone, frantically flip through apps: What did I post? Where did I post it?

I was told that I'd gone into the kitchenette at 3 a.m. and grabbed handfuls of Haribo Starmix, turned to the people in the lounge, and said, "Now is the time when the sad man eats candy in his bunk."

WHITE (2016)

I took some Ambien, slept, and woke to find that I'd been on Amazon. I'd bought an all-white outfit: white shirt, white pants, white socks, white boxers, white shoes, white belt.

DOTE
(1987, 1995, 1998, 2000, 2002)

I wore my dumb pink Replacements shirt in a Cambridge pizza shop. A guy said, "Hey, do you like the Replacements?"

I was so happy because I thought a real Replacements fan would be disgusted by my dumb pink shirt.

"You should go to the Rat tonight. There's a band there that's just like the Replacements," said the guy.

Where's the Rat?

"Kenmore Square," he said, like, *This guy lives in Boston and hasn't heard of the Rat?*

I'd heard of the Rat. Maybe the CBGB of Boston? But I was sixteen and had no shot at getting in.

"They're called the Lemonheads," said the guy, who years later I would realize was Evan Dando. "They're really great. They sound just like the Replacements."

As we left with the pizza, Evan Dando called after me, "Remember! The Rat! The Lemonheads! Just like the Replacements!"

From that day, I was cosmically fated to bump into Evan Dando. I saw him at shows and at bars. I dated a dominatrix who was writing a book—as roughly 80 percent of dominatrixes are writing a book—who lived in his building. I saw him at the Angelika Film Center once, at a showing of *Hideous Kinky*. I saw him at Brownies, on Avenue A in the East Village, entirely by himself at the front of the stage, clapping and hooting for a band made up of runway models.

Soul Coughing played Glastonbury after our first album came out in the UK. We stayed at one of the two hotels in London that all bands stay at—I can't remember the name of the one we were at, but the other one was the Columbia. We were at the curb with our instruments.

Evan Dando strolled up and started talking as if the conversation had been in progress.

"Are you guys a band?" asked Evan Dando.

"No," said our keyboard player, and walked away.

Yes, I said. I almost mentioned the pizza shop, but had the sense that if I talked about my band, I would have to stand there while he talked about his band.

"What's your name?"

Doughty.

"Dough-tee? Dote-tee? Do they call you that because you *dote* on young girls?" He was swaying a little.

He was followed by an older woman in groovy-kid clothes. She had a leathery tan and stiff hair. I didn't know why she was following Evan Dando. I was terrified of getting into a conversation with her.

I read later that she was Anita Pallenberg, the model who'd left Brian Jones for Keith Richards during a drive through Morocco. I'd had a picture of her and Keith Richards, whom I revered, on my wall at school.

Soul Coughing played a tertiary stage at 11:15 a.m. All bands had a record company angling to get them on the bill at Glastonbury, so there were too many bands, on too many stages. Nonstop, starting in the morning. Before us was 311, at 10:45. Skunk Anansie was on at 11:45.

Irritated hippies emerged from pup tents. A remarkable number of people want to camp at festivals in the cold English summer, trudge in mud strewn with cigarette butts and lager glasses, eat curries bought from parked RVs.

I looked up *evan dando glastonbury.* The first result was *Lemonheads' Evan Dando Relives Lowest Moment.* He was wasted, very late, and delayed Portishead, who in 1995 were the favorite band of everyone in Britain.

They pelted him with trash.

"They put us on when all our fans had left," says Dando in the interview.

The journalist interviewing him claimed to have been among those booing.

ADDENDUM ON DANDO

My tone in the preceding piece: I scorn him for his beauty. He's so beautiful that Anita Pallenberg followed him around!

A high percentage of *anybody* who's written about Evan Dando insist he has no right to have a problem with it. Because being gorgeous is his brand.

Is it? How is that a calculation? Such a weird way to be awful to someone.

Kathleen Hanna—an icon, a pioneer who truly made music better—wrote, in her twenties, a tortured zine called *My Life with Evan Dando*. It expresses—so finely—what it is to hate someone because you're attracted to them. One page is a Xeroxed collage of Evan Dando with the text *I am as evil* [sic].

An enduring shame among musicians from the 1990s is what dicks we were to each other. I should say, some of us were. Many of us were.

DIGGER (1995)

I was at the stage the Lemonheads played on at Glastonbury—not for them, or Portishead, but hours before, to see Billy Bragg.

He was twenty minutes late. An impatient guy with a lager hollered, "Come on, Bragg! Come on!"

I'd never seen him; never had any friends that were fans. Here I was in a crowd of strangers yelling along to "Little Time Bomb." He played "Levi Stubbs' Tears" and the whole audience joyfully sang the trombone solo.

He played "The World Turned Upside Down." I'd never heard it. How can I have been a Billy Bragg fan and never heard it? But I was.

It was like falling into a tunnel. My whole body was gooseflesh. I've been trying to imitate that maniacal guitar line since the day after that show.

The world was absolutely new.

MILES (2004)

I used to get upgraded to business class because I flew a certain number of yearly miles. A brief heyday: United soon put fees between me and the large chair in the sky.

I needed a thousand to get the large chair for another year. I looked for a destination: Vegas was cheap to fly to on Christmas Eve. I'm not a gambler, so I could get in and out and not be broke.

I got a decent room at the Palms for almost nothing. The Palms had a certain credibility with me because the twelfth season of *The Real World* was shot there.

I got into the room and switched the TV on. On Christmas, MTV would suspend its reality-show brand and for twenty-four hours be the MTV of 1986: vintage Christmas bumpers and novelty videos, my favorite being Bryan Adams's "Reggae Christmas" featuring Pee-wee Herman in a dreadlock wig.

Retro-MTV Christmas and room-service chicken: a fine holiday.

That was the year they ditched retro Christmas. On MTV, there was a teen standing in a Californian cul-de-sac. He got into an RV and was taken on a date or something.

There was a Coffee Bean & Tea Leaf by the casino floor.

You're not going to be open tomorrow, right? I asked the barista. She was puzzled. "Why wouldn't we be open?"

I went to the Strip and wandered around fake Rome, fake Egypt, and fake Italy.

I went to a strip club and got a lap dance from a chatty stripper who had a deft way of briefly touching my dick and nonchalantly mentioning the Champagne Room.

I wore a black Paul Smith suit: three buttons, notched lapel, English cut, purple lining. A little bit too close to a Vince Vaughn move, but it was a nice suit. I was the only person I saw wearing a suit in Vegas except behind a check-in desk.

"I thought you were a limo driver," said the lap dancer.

In the cab back to the hotel, the driver said, "Isn't it weird that it's Christmas?"

If you live here, shouldn't it just *be* Christmas?

I woke up on Christmas Day and went to the casino floor. Elderly women sat at the slot machines pressing buttons— *blum blim blunk* sounds. Bleary-looking, like they'd been there all night.

I went to fake France, fake Camelot, and the fake Arctic, which had no white tigers because one had recently mauled Roy. I went to a steak house and was suckered into ordering what the waiter called *the number-one cut of meat in Vegas right now.*

I went to a different strip club that night. An anxious stripper with white-pleather skin kept returning to my table, saying, "Do you want a lap dance? Do you want a lap dance?"

I courteously demurred. She gave me a look like, *You're wasting my time!* Then she'd come back ten minutes later.

One stripper had a French accent. I succumbed to the Champagne Room.

Instantly there was a bottle of champagne. I freaked out: I'm sober. The stripper was gracious, had the waitress take the bottle and replace it with strawberries.

Is it worth your time for me to tell you I never go to strip clubs? It's not.

Soon they brought a credit-card machine on a silver plate, and I was being told how much for the strawberries, the diet cola; it's customary to tip, *but only if you want to.*

I didn't want to be the guy who balks. I was out $1,200.

The bathroom attached to the Champagne Room was as bright and cold as a Whole Foods.

My custom earned me a ride in their white limo. The driver took a side street, past loading docks. I tipped him extravagantly: I wanted to feel like a meaningful person.

DRAPES (2006)

We played next to a cheesesteak spot in Philly. They put Cheez Whiz on them. People who haven't been to Philly don't believe it, but it's delightful.

I went out the club's back door into an alley. Four women stood by the tour bus. Three of them, overjoyed, handed the fourth their camera.

I said to the fourth woman, Is there something you want signed? She was incredulous.

Maybe I said something weird?

I asked, Do you—want a picture?

Her eyes widened: I'd insulted her? My default is: I'm wrong. But I didn't know what I'd said. Have we met before?

"No?" she said, like, *What are you asking?*

Have we—communicated—?

"Yes," she said, bewildered. "Of course we have."

Like—what?

"All *kinds* of nice things," she said.

She stared in disbelief.

I don't remember the excuse, but I ran back to the dressing room, clapped open my laptop, frantically scanned MySpace—that was my mood-changer, flirting with strangers on MySpace—and my emails.

I didn't see her. I scanned again. Still didn't see her.

"Is this a joke?" she said when I came back.

I could not process this woman, neatly dressed in mall clothes, being delusional. I understand some hallucinations: a face or a voice. I can even empathize with de Clérambault's syndrome: a woman thought the arrangement of drapes in Buckingham Palace were coded messages from the king.

I can't imagine someone hallucinating an extended interaction on MySpace.

I said, I have to get a cheesesteak.

I took off down the alley.

"I came all the way to Philly!" she yelled at my back.

The door was locked. I saw a guy in a paper hat spraying the grill with blue fluid. Then the sign blinked off. Somebody at the counter saw me and unlocked the door.

"We ran out of bread," she said apologetically.

My phone rang.

"Hi, this is Chuck," Chuck said. "You may know me from such films as *I'm Your Tour Manager* and *Where Are You, the Bus Is Leaving*."

LYRE (2007)

Alley lady emailed months later.

The subject line of the first email was: *Krar*.

The second: *KRAR*.

The third: *Krarrrrrrrrrrrrrrr*.

The krar is an East African instrument: an electric lyre. I'd gone to Eritrea and blogged my search for one—I found traditional krars and krars that looked like Dimebag Darrell's guitar sawed in half and then glued into krar-shape.

She'd hallucinated a motif: jokes about the word *krar*. Creepy, because this is *exactly* my kind of inside joke.

I blocked her. I remembered: be boring.

A week passed. She wrote from a new address: *Krarkrarkrarkrar*.

I blocked. From a new email address: *Kraaaarkrraaaaaar*.

Blocked again. From another new address: *Krrrrrrrararararararararar*.

In exasperation I replied: *I have not emailed you. I do not know you. Please do not email me.*

You can tell I am cold and neutral because I am not using contractions.

What a fool: I took the bait. But she stopped.

I AM THINKING OF YOUR VOICE
(1989)

I was wandering up Dumaine Street, in New Orleans, looking for breakfast. My dad's family is in Tullos, Louisiana; we were visiting—we stopped in New Orleans before we flew home.

The night before, I'd bumped into my middle school bully: Jimmy Damron. He used to call me *dil-Doughty*, and his laughing henchmen—among them Skip Gill, who had forsaken me—pretended they got the joke. But we were both nineteen now; we walked for hours together around the French Quarter. It hadn't occurred to us that someone surely sells alcohol without carding.

On Decatur Street—which was deserted—a pack of high school girls came up to us and yelled in unison, "YOU ARE THE SUN-SHINE OF MY LIFE!"

They marched off except for one, who pointed an accusing finger, said, "YOU!" and ran.

I found a diner: the Clover. A gay diner, with a countdown chalkboard: *237 days 'til Mardi Gras!*

Their jukebox was a nickel per song. A nickel! I shoved every coin I had into it: Del Shannon, the Everly Brothers, Billy Squier, Soft Cell, Bo Diddley, the Bobby Fuller Four, Desmond Dekker, James Brown.

I ate at the counter; the guy wouldn't let me not have my coffee refilled. Another? No thanks. *Aw, come on!*

I walked out iridescent from caffeine.

There was a sound system in the intersection: ridiculous low end. The bassline to "Tom's Diner"—those two ominous notes— boomed over the street. A high, cold beam of synthesizer cut through it.

A friend called "Tom's Diner" a novelty tune, which shocked me: it's so scary. That bassline, the menacing strings, the vocal slowed down so slightly—you can just barely hear something strange in the texture. The way it slows down ever so slightly more for *I am thinking of your voice*; it's like when you're on acid and someone says something innocuous and a whole sinister world of suggestion emanates.

A spaceship cruised over the street, dragging a tail of fog. All the people in the intersection seemed to slow down, like they were pushing through water.

The world was absolutely new.

DRAGS (1996, 2000, 2007, 2010)

I've played the Portuguese city of Porto an unusual number of times. Everybody else plays Lisbon. I know a guy who insists he saw me in Lisbon in 1999: no memory of it.

My first time in Porto was an unexpectedly fantastic Soul Coughing show. The audience was banging on the stage with their hands. Every time I go back, people come tell me they were at that show. Nobody's forgotten it. I've met more people in Porto who've been to that show than could've possibly been at that show.

The second time was a poetry festival. Only in Europe do you get flown in, put up, and treated as an honored guest by *a poetry festival*.

I read from an epic piece called *The Lamb and Wolf Will Chill and Party*. Every time I finished a verse, I balled up the paper and threw it into the audience. They scrambled to catch it.

The third time, I went because my friend Peter Mack married a Portuguese woman—actually, they married at city hall, in Manhattan, then they went back to Portugal for a wedding party at a stately stucco mansion in Amendoeira. Peter's friends flew in from New York, and his wife Mari's from Barcelona, where she'd lived.

Both groups met at a rental car place and waited for Mari's friend who was renting the car.

I saw a woman walking down the street toward the rental place. She had strawberry-blond hair and a dark, serene expression. She was walking with a lanky man.

With my whole self, I hated him; I hated the injustice of the world, felt surging anger that she was with him and not me.

It turned out the longhaired man was one of Mari's Barcelona friends. They were just walking.

I spent the whole ride through the Portuguese countryside looking at the back of her head, too nervous to start a conversation.

I buttonholed Peter when we got to the country house. He told me she lived with a man she'd been with since she was a teenager. They split and un-split again and again: a tragic loop.

I still made sure I sat near her.

I'm allergic to fish. I asked her to teach me how to say "Is there fish in this?" in Portuguese. It led to a funny, easy conversation.

There were nonstop courses: tiny plates of food, followed by tiny drinks, followed by a tiny plate of a different delicacy, followed by a tiny glass of a different type of alcohol. Men in traditional fuzzy-Muppet costumes—pom-pom strands flopping from their arms—gallumphed into the party and harassed the bride's family, making them dance, tousling their hair.

I turned to her and said, "So, do you want to fly to Thailand and live on the beach with me forever?"

It was a joke but of course it wasn't a joke.

She took a slow, extremely European drag from her cigarette.

"No, Doughty," she said languorously. "I cannot. It is impossible."

I returned to Porto a fourth, a fifth, a sixth time. I've seen her every time I've been back there. When we meet it's like contact with an almost-life.

We met at an improbably stately café with gothic arches near the Fnac, on a street lined with billowing racks of discount clothes.

She was starting a nightlife magazine, which I talked her into not naming *Hipster*. Dusk blushed the windows.

There was a lull, and I said, "So, how's the dude?"

She smiled.

"The dude," she said. She dragged cinematically, then exhaled the smoke. "The dude, Doughty. The dude is fine."

VENEERS (2002)

I had this delightful, profane dentist who wanted me to get massive, gleaming Erik Estrada veneers—so I could sing on the Super Bowl.

He wasn't upselling: he thought it would happen.

I was two years clean; my mouth was fucked. I went back, and I went back, and I went back. The high whine of the drill made me a wobbling mess.

The dentist—a sober guy—finally said, "Take the gas."

They strapped the pig-nose on; the gas whooshed in the tube; I dissociated by degrees.

"Are you fucking seeing god yet?" asked my dentist.

A curtain of undulating beads descended on the world. I decided I was going to enjoy it. Then I heard the radio in the next room—the lite-rock station.

"I want to know what love is. I want you to show me," sang Lou Gramm.

PUNTING (2007)

My shrink was a wizard-bearded man with a Texas accent. His office smelled like moldy Freon. Next to his diploma was child's art, something of a shrink's coat of arms: crying face, couch, box of tissues, happy face.

I'd had unpredictable results from meds: this guy got it right. I was his patient for three years. I was touring, so he'd call in prescriptions wherever I was.

Sometimes he made mistakes: the dosages, the spelling of my name.

A pharmacist in San Diego said he was expecting me to be seventy. I was born in 1970—did you hear it wrong?

"No, your doctor said you were seventy years old."

The errors became more frequent.

It became comic ritual: a pharmacy got it wrong, but I was leaving town; they punted to another pharmacy, which also got it wrong, and punted it to the next town.

I had to keep calling him.

"This happens every time," he said. "You can't make me do this anymore."

I repeated what the pharmacists said. He angrily told me, no, he'd told them the right prescription, who are these pharmacists you find?

In sessions he was blurting out things shrinks don't say to patients.

"You should get married soon," he said out of nowhere.

What?

241

"You don't want to get old with a woman you didn't know when she was young and attractive."

The last time he fucked up a prescription, I didn't want to deal, so I let the med run out. I crashed into depression and anxiety.

I called my therapist, who was baffled—she'd known him a long time. She got me a new doctor.

Two months later she told me the Texan wizard had died of lung cancer. She didn't know he was sick: he'd had it for years but wouldn't give up his practice. He'd been fading out as the disease progressed and the painkillers increased.

PRIME (2015)

I ditched Cymbalta. I'd just broken up with _____ and moved far away; what could go wrong?

Cymbalta commercials were a sad pebble that can't make friends until it takes Cymbalta. My story was that the pebble took Cymbalta, briefly felt slightly better, then the pebble thought, *This isn't worth it, what do I need this for?* and tossed it. Then the pebble cried at all stimuli.

There was an Amazon commercial on which a UPS guy in a Broadway musical sings, "There's more to Prime!"

I burst into tears.

I started doing a thing with a friend: every day we text each other something we're grateful for. It can be one word: *sunset, coffee, dog.*

USUAL (2005)

There was a street-marketing campaign in 1995: posters in Manhattan that said *WHO IS KEYSER SÖZE?* Also on posters that year: *WHO IS REVS?* (an artist), *WHERE IS COMEDY CENTRAL?* (channel 45 on Time Warner Cable), *WHO'S DOWN WITH O.P.P.?* (yeah, you know: me).

I decided not to see *The Usual Suspects*.

It alarmed Scrap—seriously, *alarmed* him—that I hadn't seen it. He went to a Target somewhere on the road and bought the DVD.

We were opening for Barenaked Ladies in hockey arenas. Every night we played a forty-minute set; we sat on the bus for the rest of the time. In parking garages beneath the ice.

Our tour manager had been nicknamed Fudge by the drummer—for finessing crises with mild lying.

"Anybody want to watch this?" said Fudge, holding up Scrap's DVD.

I was in the kitchenette with Cashmere Dan, eating our delicacy: the hate-a-dilla. Supermarket pre-sliced Swiss between tortillas, melted in a microwave.

That's okay, Fudge.

Fudge came out of the lounge two hours later. "You've all seen *The Usual Suspects*, right?"

I haven't, actually.

"I can't believe Kevin Spacey was Keyser Söze!"

Pause.

I *just told you* I haven't seen it.

"I thought you were joking!" he said. With a look of real shock.

Have I ruined it for somebody? I carry the curse.

"But you're going to watch it someday—you will, right?" Scrap asks.

EACH LOUD MIGHTY (2001)

I got clean and toured alone: drove thousands of miles to dozens of cities. Desperate not to be in Soul Coughing—or in a Soul Coughing cover band.

My receptors were burnt out. My only functioning act of creativity was journaling—psychotic entries, prayerful or nonsensical. New songs were sad misfires; about nothing. Not the syllabic-collage nothing that I'm known for: these had no core.

The words banged into each other like the robots in the demolition derby in *A.I.*

On September Eleventh, I wrote a single, mournful line: "Call me back when the war is over."

_____ used to tend bar near the World Trade Center, serving drunk finance-industry workers. I didn't know if she could call me back—did a building fall on her?

I bought a $30 background check on the internet: she was still alive in Jersey City.

She had this beguiling, unusual name: I struggled to cram it into a melody. Or coax a melody out of it. No dice. Half the songs on *Haughty Melodic* began as attempts to sing _____'s name. The closest I got was a song called "Unsingable Name."

In one, I pleaded with her: *I'm not worth a dime, I'll drag you down, don't waste your time.*

Hard sell: don't love me.

I turned to the psychotic journaling. I copied fragments into a separate notebook, locating a sense of yearning. Coaxing out the phrases with that affinity: yearning, yearning, yearning.

I was getting up at five to watch the light come on—I was all about the light—and write guitar parts as I drank coffee. I laid the phrases harvested from journals over the guitar parts like rails onto crossbars.

DAYLIGHT ECHO UM

I found the title before the songs. I entered *Michael Doughty* into an anagram generator; among the results was *Haughty Melodic.*

ACIDLY HUGE MOTH (2002)

I went to Dan Wilson's house in Minneapolis to write a bridge for "Busting Up a Starbucks," not realizing we'd be making *Haughty Melodic* for four years.

I found Dan because we were both working with somebody who was—I didn't realize at the time—weirdly disconnected. He suggested we work together because there wasn't anybody else he could get in touch with.

It was tremendous luck.

Dan and I didn't touch the bridge to "Busting Up a Starbucks" but wrote the beginnings of two songs in one day.

GAUCHO DELI MYTH

I came back to Minneapolis to finish those two songs. We buttoned them up fast, and I started showing him other songs.

Dan talked me into what I thought were bad ideas. The skeleton of one tune had a lifting turnaround that landed on the home chord with *In your long, black American car.*

"There are so many songs where the most interesting part of the song is a throwaway at the end of a chorus," he said.

I tried to prove to him that it was supposed to be what it was. But when we expanded the part—making it the chorus—the song was real.

HALTED YOGI CHUM

We saw there was an album here.

I thought it would be a whole-grain process: some piano, Wurlitzer, acoustic guitar, percussion, Dan singing harmonies. Done in a month, schedule permitting.

HI MY GHOUL ACTED

I brought in most of the *Haughty Melodic* songs as mystery blobs.

Dan would locate some intuitive part of it; found facets to scrape out and polish.

The songs pulled into sharp focus.

I kept telling him chord changes were a bad idea; Dan prevailed. I never wrote bridges; Dan knows how a bridge can be an accumulator of momentum for the coda.

That's working with a real producer.

My role in the push-pull was insisting that the drums could stay on one simple pattern—trances.

Dan's style winds back to the Beatles; mine winds back to the hip-hop records that wind back to James Brown.

HELIUM YACHT DOG (2003)

We recorded in his third-floor studio. Amps were in closets; a tiny bedroom fit the drum kit. His wife insisted on a house with a third floor because she didn't want him in a basement all day. On the old architectural plans, the third floor was noted as: *BALLROOM*.

The cables were on labeled pegs, the guitars were neatly lined on stands, the piano was immaculately tuned. Dan sat at the computer on a blue yoga ball.

I flew to Minneapolis from wherever I was when I was touring—whenever Dan had the time and I had the airfare. We called in friends—John Munson on bass, Jay Rodriguez on saxophone, Eric Fawcett from N.E.R.D. on drums—to overdub parts; each part solved a problem and created two problems.

We wrote to-dos on a whiteboard in the ballroom: a list that was longer whenever I left. So I had to come back.

CAD THY HUGE LIMO

The guest room I slept in was also on the third floor. I would wake up in the darkness, go to the whiteboard, and gape incredulously at the ever-lengthening list.

CAGED HOMILY HUT

I'd been doing this routine with Dan's daughter Coco during her snack time: make the devil sign and go, *Rock and roll! Yeah!*

She made the devil sign and said, "Rockity roll!!"

Every time I came back to Dan's house to knock the next few items off the whiteboard in the ballroom, Coco would see me, make the devil sign, and go, "Hi, Mike! Rockity roll!! Aaaaaaaaaaaaaah!!"

There was a rhythm to our working days in Minneapolis: we were both up at dawn and worked with monkish efficiency; at noon we went to French Meadow on Lyndale and had tempeh Reubens.

Then we'd get into the three o'clock detail: some minor flaw that Dan spent hours chasing.

Dan bristled at my jokes about the three o'clock detail, but every day at three I'd look at my watch and he'd be choosing between five tambourines or meticulously correcting a single guitar note.

We ate dinner and went back into the ballroom firing on all cylinders again.

Between dinner and the potent evening shift I watched *Sponge-Bob* with Coco. She's a special-needs kid. She can become enraged by her confusion. But there is something uncannily happy about her: she's light in the world—an emanation of the perfection of the cosmos.

HALOED ITCHY MUG

I made an EP of the songs that Dan hadn't been crazy about. I made it fast and cheap: rinky-tink drum machines; one guitar rather than intricate layers of guitar.

Pat Dillett and I recorded it in one day. I made him do major surgery on the song "Ossining"—chopping and relocating a verse to make it a chorus—when he was running late to meet his wife.

"Why can't we do this tomorrow?"

Recording in one day was important.

He mixed the next. The complicated aspect was that I wanted every song slightly sped up or slowed down—ever so slightly. That's easy on a tape machine, less easy on Pro Tools—at least in 2004. I wanted a trace of uncanniness—and to baffle musicians trying to parse out the guitar parts.

I self-released it—preceding *Haughty Melodic* though it was made when we'd been working on *Haughty Melodic* for years.

I titled it *Rockity Roll*. In the credits, I put *Bodhisattva: Coco*.

DO HUGE MYTHICAL

A bodhisattva is one who attains enlightenment but stays in the world to help others.

ACHE HID GLUM TOY

Dan had a DVD of the Beatles' *Ed Sullivan* debut in real time: commercials, other acts, everything. I watched it on my laptop as he set up mics.

The sponsor was Excedrin. One commercial was a monstrous clock and a voiceover: "Eight o'clock: pain. Nine o'clock: pain. Ten o'clock: pain. Eleven o'clock: pain."

Davy Jones of the Monkees was on the show, in the cast of *Oliver!* Why isn't this basic trivia we learn about the Monkees or the Beatles? It's exactly how an old world became a new one.

Frank Gorshin did impressions. I'd known him only as the Riddler on the 1960s *Batman*. He wore a tuxedo. The audience went hysterical at his Dean-Martin-is-drunk bit. How sweet to win them—most were there for the Beatles.

The Beatles' second song was "Till There Was You" from *The Music Man*—you know, Harold Hill, Marian the librarian, trouble in River City. They hastened into it, barely letting "All My Loving" ring out. They must've been anxious to placate adults.

CLOTHE HIM GAUDY

I spieled my way into first class on Northwest. I was headed to Minneapolis for a week with Dan; I was listening to rough mixes on a Sony Discman.

A dazzling girl—late teens?—was in front of me. She carried a superfluity of shopping bags—Lanvin, Bergdorf, Chanel, Saks—like she was the St. Pauli Girl.

She sat. I could see between the seats: I was mesmerized by the tiny blond hairs on her arm.

An elderly man came down the aisle. A *truly* elderly man. He struggled to walk but held a stiff posture, trying to look like he wasn't working to do so. He wore expensive young-rich-dude clothes; what hair he had was combed over into a proto-Bieber.

His fake teeth were massive and white as an iPod out of the box. The sleeves of his Merino cardigan were pulled up; the sagging flesh of his arms, speckled with liver spots, swung when he moved.

He sat next to the girl with the mesmerizing tiny arm-hairs and held her hand.

He took out an iPod. The newest one—no click wheel, but touch-sensitive. I wanted to know what he was listening to; I leaned toward the crack between chairs. I expected him to be listening to opera—something that rich elderly men in movies seek respite in.

I saw the iPod screen: it was "Sexual (Li Da Di)" by Amber.

The teenage concubine: embarrassing. A man in his—eighties? Nineties? Yes, he was that old—doing the hair, wearing the clothes: a nightmare. But struggling to enjoy Euro house? A gulf of pitch-black horror.

I know that sounds like a punch line, but when I think of that old man listening to that song I'm overwhelmed by osmotic shame.

DICE YUM LOT HA (2004)

I burned the newest version of *Haughty Melodic* onto a CD-R and took it to Bonnaroo.

I was playing with a great band that I didn't know how to use. I hadn't figured out a balance between improvisatory impulses and the arrangement jiujitsu I was learning from Dan. The band weren't digging it.

My old friend Ani DiFranco came to my stage to check it out and stayed for a song and a half.

Bonnaroo had a laminate system based on the names of its stages: *Who, Where, Which, What, Why, How*. The highest echelon was *Infinity*. I didn't have *Infinity*, and I didn't know anybody who'd do me a solid and spot me one. *What* or *Why*, maybe; not *Infinity*.

Bonnaroo didn't let bands' vehicles on-site: many complexities of cross-loading gear onto tractor-pulled flatbeds while musicians were shifted around on a golf-cart-based public-transport system. But the complexity opened wormholes into the forbidden realms.

I found Dave Matthews in the land of *Infinity*. He'd liked Soul Coughing and lobbed some opportunities to us. We opened for him at Madison Square Garden. I came out to do a freestyle during his set—out of my mind on MDMA.

The first thing Dave said to me was, "'27 Jennifers' is genius!"

A song on *Rockity Roll* about how there were so many high school kids with the same name in the 1980s. It could've been Lisas, Brians, or Amys.

HEY CHAD GUM TOIL

Dave's label, ATO, would put out *Haughty Melodic*.

The triumph: nothing new added to the whiteboard. The list would get shorter—then there'd be no list!

The bridge to "Busting Up a Starbucks" was one of the last things we did.

We were layering a strangulated noise—the percussionist Ken Chastain had emailed the sample to us—into the coda. Was it a snake-charmer's flute? A ship's horn? We realized we'd never gotten around to the bridge.

We spliced a few bars into the middle of the song; came up with some chords—a build, a burst into the head progression. Dan threw me onto the microphone to improvise something to build out from.

Dan had made fun of one of my go-to moves: using city names as evocative devices. I had picked it up from a teacher, the poet Sekou Sundiata, who had a profound influence on how I approach making art. When the track kicked in, I yelled—impulsive lark— *Nyack! Ronkonkoma! East Orange! Piscataway!*

Dan sat on his blue yoga ball laughing.

"Does that work?" I asked, surprised.

"I'll buy it," he said.

HUE ALMIGHTY DOC

Dan and I sat in the dim kitchen listening to the final mixes. What a sweet moment: we were laughing together. It was so special: the album and the friendship.

DIM HOTLY GAUCHE (2005)

I played on *Letterman* again.

I did a smile and a nod when he shook my hand this time.

I played a benefit for WFUV with Rosanne Cash. She said during her show, "It's intimidating playing with a great songwriter like Mike Doughty."

Rosanne Cash said that!

People took the album into their hearts, their lives: they've named children after songs on *Haughty Melodic*, danced their first dance at weddings to its songs, learned its songs to sing at friends' memorial services.

I played First Avenue in Minneapolis on the tour supporting *Haughty Melodic*. I stayed at Dan's. At some point in the night I thought, *Tomorrow we can edit the guitar on "Madeline."*

FAKE NAMES (2012)

After my first book came out, I got a text from _____, with the unsingable name.

How dare you say ____ and not talk about ____? How could you say ____ when you didn't mention _____?

I wrote about all of those things, I replied, confused.

I found a copy and texted her the page numbers.

Like most people who are told they're in a book, she didn't read the book but flipped through, looking for herself.

In fact, I'd been forced by the lawyer to change so many details about her that she—more than anyone else in the book—seemed fictional to me: fictional job, fictional characteristics.

I got emails from people angry about details I'd fucked up: I said she was tall, she wasn't that tall, and she was sensitive about her height; I said he knew CPR, actually he was a real EMT; I said she was from Holland, she was from France.

I deeply regret the mistakes. I'm really sorry.

I had no axes to grind. Really. I was telling stories because I thought they were good stories.

Fake names were the weirdest part. I came up with fake names for my ex-bandmates in Soul Coughing but they seemed so ludicrous that instead I called them the instruments they played. This was perceived as a slight. Actually, I wish I'd done something like that for everybody and not used any fake names.

The fake names in the first draft weren't good enough for the lawyer. I had to change them if they had the same first letter, or rhymed, or suggested a clue.

He flagged the name of a music-business guy for not being fake enough.

I told him the guy was dead.

"A lawyer loves to hear that," he said.

FABULISM (2018)

About _____, in the beginning of the book—the woman I met in the park who had stories I didn't remember: she is empathetic and funny. She has fiery gifts both as an artist and an observer of art. I treasure her with all of my heart. I'm saying this because there was no trace of these feelings in my first book. It was shocking and hurtful to her.

I gave her a pseudonym in the book.

"McMuffin, Maguffin? I can't even remember it. Who is that person?" she says.

After the park—when I told her about the stories in the book— she was dismayed but didn't rush to read it. Then she was warned by a friend: "There's no love in it."

She was shocked by the coldness of the tone.

"But there was so much *play,*" she said.

I interviewed her for *this* book; my plan was to run it verbatim. It would've been thirty pages.

The interview reminded me of something we did when we were kids: videotape our conversation, then watch it, making observations, fascinated with ourselves. The camcorder doubled as our VCR, so we couldn't videotape the conversation about that conversation. We surely would have.

By coincidence, right before we met for that interview, she found a box in her mom's house: ephemera from our relationship, postcards and notes. There *was* a lot of play: I wrote to her the most loving things.

I told her that what I wrote in those notes and postcards was absolutely real. Because it was.

The most confusing part to her was the absence of my voice as she remembered it. Before the interview, she listened to the audiobook.

I cringed.

"When I listened to it, there you were. I could hear you, I heard *you*, and you were *you* as I know you," she said.

She was curious about one part I surely remembered but didn't include: as a kid, I was a fabulist. I invented experiences and told them as my tales. I've been ashamed of those lies—the fabulism—since I got over it. Which was in my early twenties. Too old to be a fabulist.

As I type this, I can't feel my hands—my heart is racing—I want to hide my face.

I remain deeply ashamed.

"But they were *stories*," she said, surprised by the depth of my shame. "You wanted to *tell* stories."

AN ADD (2009)

I got a MySpace add from a Japanese band called Uhnellys. A duo: Kim, a bass player with a stately and delicate Afro, and a drummer who called herself Midi—not after the interface between digital instruments but the French word for noon.

Kim rapped like Wile E. Coyote running off a cliff.

Midi played like Jabo Starks in a noise-rock band.

I love your music, I wrote.

Kim wrote back in flawed English that he idolized me.

You should take me on tour in Japan, I wrote back. Being funny.

Six months later he'd booked twenty shows and bought plane tickets for me and Scrap.

CHANNELS

It's a fourteen-hour flight from New York to Tokyo. It feels supernatural: there's a hush after takeoff, like all passengers realize at once how long we'll be in the air.

On any flight, by the time I'm seated I think I'm in the city that I'm going to. *I'm in Tucson*, I'll text to somebody before liftoff in Chicago. Even on a transatlantic flight, I'm in Berlin when they start making announcements in German.

Not to Japan. To Japan, when you reach approximate London distance you're not halfway there.

They give you a little kit—in economy, not just in business class—with the tiny tube of toothpaste, pen for forms, earplugs: you need *supplies*.

One of the entertainment channels was a feed from the under-side of the plane. A plane on a parallel path flew beneath us—I was half-asleep and thought it was an animation. It was with us for a few minutes, then banked and flew away.

GHOST DETECTOR

When we landed in Tokyo I turned to Scrap and said, Remember the signs are all in Japanese and you need to pay close attention to not get lost.

Hey: foreshadowing.

It was during a SARS scare. People in hazmat suits, gauze booties, and masks boarded the plane, walking the aisles and spraying disinfectant.

At passport control there was a camera detecting body heat. Vague body forms—blotches of light—drifted on the monitor. Some mostly gray, some mostly white. Can they tell you have a fever before you actually feel it?

COGNITION

GHOST DETECTOR

There is a cartoon on every surface. Manic creatures crawl on all objects: manholes, stairs, doors, paper-towel dispensers, ladders, shopping carts, bathroom mirrors, cutlery.

Exploding colors everywhere.

They love the Roman alphabet just as we love kanji (I met somebody who'd gotten a *chaos* tramp-stamp when drunk; in Taiwan, a shocked woman said, "What man did this to you?" In fact, the tattoo said *livestock*). If you're a lover of fragment poetry, it's a feast:

World's Skating Player Everyone Is First
Nobody Seems To Understand The Nature
Shining Diary What You Smile
It's Splend I Don't Know Whatto Don't

Naturally your mind finds your language and tries to read it; it became disturbing—dyslexia blossoming. All walls shouting. Nowhere for eyes to rest. In cognitive exhaustion, I'd think I'd forgotten my language.

A friend of Kim's told me he saw a bouncer in London with a tattoo across his muscled chest: *NOODLES*.

SCENARIO ROCK

Scrap and I called a certain kind of Japanese act *scenario rock*. In every city we played last; Uhnellys played before us; before them were three local bands of varying genre: could be a prog band, a punk band, or a rapper. Invariably one act was a dude playing scenario rock.

At Mortar Records in Kumagaya, it was this chubby guy in wire glasses. He played delicate arpeggios, letting them ring—then he tapped once on the guitar's body—long moment of silence—and returned to gentle chords.

It might have seemed like a Zen garden—every pebble in place—but it was ridiculous.

One chorus—in English—went, *I make up scenarios. I make up scenarios. I make up scenarios.*

More Zen garden; back to *I make up scenarios. I make up scenarios. I make up scenarios.*

Tap—pause—strum—*I make up scenarios. I make up scenarios. I make up scenarios.*

Was it like that sketch-comedy thing: repeat seven times and it's funny again? It did get funny for a moment—then torturous—then funny because it was so torturous—then beyond torturous: I fell into a tunnel between dimensions.

The world was absolutely new.

WISH PADDLE

My birthday happened twice in Japan, because of the international date line. I didn't really want to celebrate two birthdays: I made a joke about it, and Kim and Midi took it seriously.

On my New York birthday we had the afternoon to kill; behind our hotel we found a road of flawless asphalt—as all asphalt in Japan is perfect—followed it, and found a temple at the end.

Kim and Midi showed us the fun temple rituals: walk across a symbolically steep bridge, do a certain number of claps at a ceremonial well, eat ceremonial candy.

We bought wooden paddles from a monk in a kiosk. You write wishes on the paddle and hang it with hundreds of other wooden paddles—other visitors' wishes.

I wrote a tormented prayer for the strength to really love my girlfriend with all of my heart—she of Cool Joe Hill the skateboarding dog.

Kim, delighted, got out a camera to take a picture.

I yelled, NO NO NO NO.

It's supposed to be fun: you wish for your grandchild's grades, or your baseball team in the playoffs.

The place struck me as a sacred Dave & Buster's.

On my Japan birthday they got a cake and sang, *Happy birthday, Mike Doughty!* Always the whole name, never just Mike.

INNOCENCE

American bands that tour Japan tell the same story: every day is plotted; you're whisked along by promoters; you're in Western hotels—you could be in Omaha—and you take the bullet train between cities.

All times precise. Not for control, but as courtesy. For one thing, to mitigate cultural delirium. Uhnellys didn't know this stuff—and the tour was wonderful. We traveled in their car, ate roadside noodles.

We stayed at a truck stop: I was afraid it'd be shared-bathroom, but the room had one of those Japanese toilets that look like Darth Vader, with cleaning jets—adjustable strength and temperature. It was a *shower* that the room lacked. The motel had an *onsen*—a hot spring, in a truck stop!

We didn't know tattoos were forbidden in *onsens*. We got shocked looks.

I goofed by loudly opening a door. Adjacent to the *onsen* were the budget accommodations: a vast, hushed space of cushions with foot-high privacy screens.

We hung out with local bands in Osaka, Yamagata, Fukuoka, eating incredible food. Alley cafés. One place was decorated with cartoons of a guy with a human head and a chicken body: the name translated to *Little Yama's House of Wings*.

THE MARS, THE CLOCK

The first two weeks of shows were never more than a hundred miles from Tokyo. Uhnellys put us up where they lived: the suburb of Kasukabe. We would drive back after shows, wake up, drive to the next town, play, return to Kasukabe.

No Japanese promoter would countenance this: it was wonderful.

Kasukabe was like the Ronkonkoma of Tokyo. So, so far from the groovyland. We loved it. Nobody would show it to a foreigner.

My friend Tadzio who lived in Tunisia told me that every American traveler wants to be the only white man in the movie. That's who we were in Kasukabe.

One night the opener was called Music from the Mars. Their guitar player was a promoter, bringing bands from K Records and Kill Rock Stars to Japan.

"Many Northwest scene," he said.

He was stunned that we were staying in Kasukabe. In the dressing room he'd say, "Kasukabe!" and laugh hysterically.

The Kasukabe hotel served breakfast obsequiously: toast and a hideous poached egg. The proprietor was deeply concerned—in a friendly way—that we'd enjoy it.

It was a grave duty. Scrap and I dreaded facing the egg. We lay in bed until the phone rang.

"Hello, time for breakfast."

Thank you, but we do not want breakfast.

"Do you want breakfast later?"

No, thank you, we do not want breakfast, thank you.

"No breakfast?"

Thank you, no, we do not want breakfast, thank you.

I don't know why eliminating contractions seems like the correct way to address a Japanese person.

We unplugged the phone before going to sleep.

We bought cloying milky coffee from vending machines. Taped to their sides were tattered posters of Japanese murderers—sabulous mug shots and severe black kanji.

Japan had a fifteen-year statute of limitations on murder (it doesn't anymore). TV ran countdowns. If they ran out the clock, fugitives emerged from hiding places, waving.

I SWORE I SAW BOSS SPORT

One brand was BOSS Coffee; the cans show a graphic of a guy who looks like David Niven—pipe in his mouth, two stark dashes indicating crow's feet.

They had dedicated machines; their current ads were Tommy Lee Jones with a *why am I here?* look.

Favorite BOSS products:

BOSS Silky Drip
Friendly BOSS
BOSS Intermission
BOSS Refreshment
Ultra BOSS
Smart BOSS
BOSS Plus One
BOSS Begin!
BOSS Rich on Rich
BOSS Legend
BOSS of the Morning

ON LOVE HOTEL HILL

We played four shows in Tokyo. An experienced promoter would consolidate—maximize draw, minimize time. Uhnellys just called the clubs they usually played, said they had this partially-famous New York person with them.

One club was on Love Hotel Hill in Shibuya. Love hotels are exceptionally common. Japan is crowded—big families live in small apartments—people need sex locations.

They are strictly zoned. On a highway—darkness on both sides of the car—you'll pass a gaudy wonderland of enticements: flashing hearts, zebra stripes. A clump of love hotels.

The audience was seated at tables. So quiet you could hear drinks being mixed.

That night's scenario-rock guy sang:

This is the only way back home
This is the only way back home
This is the only way back home
This is the only way back home
This is the only way back home
This is the only way back home
This is the only way back home

When we got onstage, there was a scrawny guy in a yellow shirt sitting on the floor in front of us. He was shitfaced. He threw up a *hell yes* fist, yelled, "ROCK AND ROLL! YEAH!"

He wasn't yelling between songs; he was polite until I sang, and then he let loose.

I swear I heard him yell, "FUCKING!"

Everyone else: silent. Jazz-club reverence.

I couldn't shut this guy down with quips—limited Japanese quip supply. It was odd to see a Japanese guy having a freak-out. I asked Kim—in gestures—to reason with him. No dice. Kim grabbed him around the torso and hauled him up.

"Wait a minute!" called an Australian voice from the darkness. "This isn't a classical concert!"

The guy flailed like a wrestler on angel dust.

"This is a rock and roll concert," continued the Australian guy in a reasonable tone. "You have to let him do what he wants."

The entire audience, other than the drunk guy and the reasonable Australian: silent.

HAD HAD HAD HAD

Kim had two questions about America:

"How do you know when you're in a 'bad neighborhood'?"

And:

"Do Americans really wear shoes in bed?"

He had seen Jennifer Aniston do it on *Friends*.

We learned some Japanese slang: *bari yabei* and *cho sagoi*, which made everybody laugh. I think we were saying something like, "Totes radical! Mad tubular!"

We tried to avoid translation knots like the English progressive tenses—the famous example sentence, *All the schooling he had had had had no effect on his intelligence*. But some stuff slipped out: the use of *ass* as a modifier, like *dope-ass noodle*—impossible to explain.

Midi sneezed. Scrap and I said, "Bless you."

Huh? We explained that you say it when somebody sneezes. I don't think they got that it wasn't a weird thing that only Scrap and I did.

Kim had a Game Boy–sized electronic dictionary: type English words; it showed Japanese definitions. I typed *bless*, then realized that made it weirder.

I wanted to know what the honorific *san* meant. I knew how it was used; I wanted to know the literal meaning. I asked Kim, who said, "Honorific."

Yes, an honorific; what does it *mean*?

He looked it up: the definition was *honorific*.

I DINED WITH THE CLOWN

When Soul Coughing played Japan in 1997, our tech Gentleman Jim called McDonald's *the embassy*.

I didn't want to go to Tokyo and eat at McDonald's. But my brain got desperate for rest: I went to the embassy.

It wasn't restful: at the counter, a girl in a maroon McDonald's uniform raised her arm in a rigid hailing gesture, yelling the traditional welcome-to-our-restaurant greeting: "いらっしゃいませ!!!!!"

We went to Denny's in Kasukabe. I read a Murakami novel where a saxophone player hangs out at Denny's: it felt defensible. Though later in the novel—perhaps in all Murakami novels—a dude makes linguine for breakfast.

It wasn't a Denny's as we knew Denny's. The menu was pictures of unidentifiable food-cubes. There was a button on the table—an emergency bell?

We flagged a waitress down—a teenager. She was dumbfounded to be flagged down. She got a manager.

The manager demonstrated—so annoyed—how to press the button, making scary eye contact with us, speaking slowly in Japanese. We weren't getting it. She spoke louder and slower, repeatedly touching the button, getting angrier that we weren't picking up what she was laying down.

We loved it.

Seafood makes me ill, so I learn variations of *Is there fish in this?* in every language. When we pressed the button and the waitress came, I tried to say 私は魚を食べることができない.

Imagine Roberto Benigni in *Down by Law* walking up to a teenage waitress and blurting, *Please I can't eat fish thank you!*

PACHINKO, CANAL

We checked into a French-themed hotel—Eiffel Tower logo—in Kyoto.

I napped and woke up an hour before sound check. It was glowing dusk. The breeze was a sigh of contentment. I took a walk.

For philosophical reasons I left my iPhone in the room.

I walked down a street of traditional houses. Easy to remember this, I thought. I came to a pachinko parlor streaked with pink neon. I made a left. At least that's what I thought I did.

Soon it was the cusp of night and about time to go to the club, the name of which I didn't know offhand. I'd put it in my iCal.

The sky got darker. I retraced my steps and discovered that at certain points where I'd visualized wider streets there were narrower ones, and tall buildings where I thought they'd be squat. I took another turn—didn't recognize anything.

I took another and found myself standing in front of a miniature temple on a plinth.

Oh, here we go, I thought. I know where I am.

A couple of turns later I was in front of the same plinth. That can't be the same plinth. Can that be the same plinth?

I didn't process that I was lost: I thought reality was at fault.

I turned randomly but each time found myself at the pachinko place.

I love the sound of pachinko parlors: steel balls banging against the pins, chaotic bells. A different digital tune screaming from each machine.

This place was closed; silent.

I peered through the grate at empty chairs in front of the machines and realized that it was a *different* pachinko parlor.

I passed monolithic apartments on a canal, television light in the windows. You know, a canal is a thing you might notice, but maybe the first time I missed the canal.

I saw a taxi! A black car with a yellow roof, lace curtains on the back windows. The driver scowled at a newspaper.

I'd heard that Japanese cab drivers pretend not to see Americans. I would have to charm him into taking me to: the Eiffel Tower? *La boulangerie, la bibliotheque, les un-deux-trois?*

I tried to open the door quietly. He threw the newspaper at the dash.

I noticed how panicked I was: flushed, sweating.

The cab smelled like baked vinyl.

Hello! Please, excuse me, thank you, I said in Japanese—exhausting my vocabulary beyond seafood—hotel, French, France hotel, *le Français, l'hotel!*

The driver nodded in slow politeness—genuinely trying to absorb what I was saying.

A tremble of panic came into my voice.

His eyebrows raised and lowered in the rearview mirror. He looked at me through the partition and said, "No?"

I repeated every affirmative or contrite Japanese word I knew. They felt fat and fake in my mouth.

He shrugged exaggeratedly—in a mean way but not in a mean way: "No? No?"

He didn't drive off when I got out of the cab. It was worse to walk away from it with the guy turning back to his newspaper.

My perspiration was suddenly very cold in the night air.

I went into a video store—I saw young people and I thought they'd be nicer. They all had the same hair: dyed beige with angular bangs.

I stood pale and bewildered at the counter. A couple of them approached me cautiously.

Excuse me—I am lost—French—hotel—name, I don't know.

There is a quick nod Japanese people do, with a blink in the middle. Like punctuation, indicating: *yep, on it.*

They walked to an old desktop computer: yellow LCD letters and a blinking square cursor. A colleague stood behind them, pointing at glowing text and clucking.

I could hear the wheels on a cart; the sound of DVD cases being reshelved. My arm-sweat pooled on the counter.

They turned the monitor toward me timidly.

There was a list of movies, all with *France* or *hotel* in the title.

I entered a fugue state.

How did I get to the police station?

STATION

The predominant sound was the buzz of fluorescent lights. There were two cops; one was a fat guy twisting his mouth as if to expel a hook. The other was a handsome man with acne scars.

I was put in a folding chair. Through a doorway I saw desks stacked with papers, surrounded by gray-scale photos, bullet-point lists with admonishing exclamation points.

I was babbling. *Music, club, Uhnellys, French, hotel.*

The handsome cop was having a hard time making sense of the distressed white man. I kept thinking he was going to pick up a phone or type something in his computer, but he just slowly repeated what of my jumbled words he could make out.

He walked away.

I'd now missed sound check—creeping closer to showtime. I put my head in my hands and rocked back and forth. The chair made a banging sound, but I couldn't stop.

The cop said something to me in the reproving way you speak to a dog; like it gets the gist. He motioned me into the office, handed me the phone.

It was Scrap.

"Mike, where are you?" his voice soft and bewildered. "We've been looking everywhere."

I told him I was at a police station and that he should hand the phone back to somebody Japanese. I realized later: I hadn't told him *why* I was at a police station.

The cop spoke briefly to whomever Scrap had handed the phone to and said, "ありがとう."

He hung up, swiveled in the chair—it squeaked—turning his back to me.

I said something like, Excuse me, hello, I'm sorry.

At first with trembling politeness, then with panic.

I tried to stop myself from hyperventilating. I was using all my strength not to climb the room like an enraged monkey.

He seemed puzzled that I wasn't satisfied.

It was showtime, and then it was *really* showtime; then I was late; then I was very late for the show. The extremely short list of reasons I've missed shows includes a forest fire and an overdose.

An hour passed.

The acne-scarred cop cocked his head, motioning me outside.

The cops were done: hit the bricks.

Such despair. Now I wander Kyoto until the angels call me home.

I felt the glass door whoosh behind me.

There was a cab idling there.

I turned to confirm the cab was for me but the cop was back inside the station.

KYOTO RULE

Kyoto rushed by the taxi's windows like Hell's Kitchen did that time I was on acid and my friend Jed drove me to a Sonic Youth show.

Kim ran outside, opened the car door, rushed me down some stairs. That's when I had the nervous collapse I was trying not to have in front of the cops. I banged the walls. I saw the dressing room—I collapsed on a chair. Trying to slow my breath.

Kim—did he know I'd come from a police station?—made an urgent, apologetic gesture.

"Now?" he said.

I maneuvered through an awkwardly quiet crowd.

My microphone was set up and my guitar was on a stand. Scrap sat with his cello, bow held at the ready. Looking bug-eyed at the crowd.

He told me he had no idea what to do. It was time to play whether I was there or not.

Now we have a Kyoto rule: if it's showtime there's a show. Somebody's in jail or abducted: there's a show.

"What would I play?" he asked. "Some of your songs I play one note for three minutes."

Have a Bach score handy? Tell jokes? Kyoto rule.

BEAMING

Scrap and Kim expressed affection by punching each other in the arm and giggling. It was adorable.

During the last sound check, Midi played a hi-hat part that was like, *tssss-tssss-mmm-bok!* Kim started playing along. "Super Bon Bon."

I hadn't done the song in years. But okay. I got up onstage and sang it with them.

I got a lesson in what a great bass player Sebastian Steinberg is—Kim was playing the right notes in the right place, but it still wasn't right—I tried to show him but immediately realized there was no way to explain it.

They were beaming.

帰る

A flight from Tokyo to New York—crossing the date line—
arrives an hour before it left.

CENTRAL (2014)

Maggie Estep kept me sober by being awake and alive in the world. She was happy. I wanted—as they say—what she had.

She died of a heart attack at age fifty. She was walking her dog and had what she thought was a panic attack. Her boyfriend insisted they go to the emergency room. She fell to the floor, went into a coma, never woke up. She'd been sober for thirty years, was a vegan for twenty, taught yoga. There was probably some cardiac flaw from her biological parents. She'd never met them.

The day can change at any time.

I was at Grand Central Station, headed up to Nyack to meet a manager. I got an email from Todd Colby—her fellow *MTV Unplugged* poet, from that weird moment in 1993 when MTV ran black-and-white films of poetry.

Todd had come from Iowa with a band called Drunken Boat. He'd sung my favorite opening lyric of all time: *Get off the tractor! Get on the bale!*

Before opening the email, I was just happy to see his name in my inbox after so long.

I wandered around Grand Central—dissociated—forgetting my train.

PINE

Maggie's funeral was at a nightclub called Helsinki, in Hudson.

I was late. I sped up the Taconic: limit fifty-five.

The state trooper was amused that I'd jammed past doing seventy-five.

I didn't say I was late for a funeral. I showed him an SBA card given to me by a friend who's NYPD in the Bronx. He was not impressed.

Scrap was a yellow cab driver; his SBA card worked with NYPD if it was presented in a specific sequence—after he rolled down the window, before he handed over his license. Each cop told Scrap the same thing: "Buy your buddy a steak dinner!"

I got to the funeral as the coffin was lowered into the grave.

It was a pine box, which was Maggie's longtime wish.

Someone put a pack of Trident on the lid.

My rental car was a soda can. It stalled on a snowy incline. I had to drift backward down the hill—bumping on drifts like a pinball—and ask the gravediggers to move their truck.

A ridiculous graveside conversation: "We'd have to back it up to the gate. Can you take it up that hill over there? Why would they rent you a car like that in the winter?"

The memorial service was packed with those whom Maggie had gotten sober or kept sober. So many of us.

Maggie's pit bull was led onstage. He circled, then lay down at the mic stand. Someone read an obituary for Lou Reed that Maggie had written for the *Voice*; she wrote that she'd never considered a world without Lou Reed in it.

I sang a song called "Day by Day By."

I talked about how she'd seen a sign near JFK and had contacted the organization it advertised: the Federation of Black Cowboys. Everybody laughed: they knew this Maggie story.

Steve Buscemi read an email from a week before she passed. He'd optioned her novel about a murder-solving hotwalker—someone who cools down a horse after racing. It concluded with Maggie's wry—but quite bald—appeal that he move to Hudson and let her be his real estate agent because she was broke and needed the commission.

Very Maggie. Big laughs.

Stephin Merritt had been her neighbor on East Fifth Street—she had listened through the floor as he recorded the Magnetic Fields' *69 Love Songs*. This stuff just happened to Maggie.

He sang "The Book of Love," possibly the greatest love song ever written—not the 1958 tune by the Monotones, but his own, which begins with the lines: *The book of love is long and boring— no one can lift the damn thing*. I named my first memoir, *The Book of Drugs*, in reference to it.

He played the ukulele and wept. Maggie's dog slept at his feet.

There was a buffet next to a grade-school photo of Maggie: in pigtails! Maggie had been *a child*?

Fire dancers performed in the parking lot.

I found myself talking to Steve Buscemi, my fellow eulogist. It's a queasy feeling, having a fan moment at a funeral. I pulled back. That thing began to happen where when someone withdraws the other becomes solicitous. I stopped hearing what he was saying because a chunk of my thoughts was so happy to be talking to Steve Buscemi and another chunk was mortified that I could enjoy it.

I said I had to run, had to split; I felt this peculiar sense of him being unconsciously needy, the way one does, like, *Wait, not yet, don't go*.

I drove the soda can back down the Taconic, thinking about how funny it would be to Maggie that I got busted for speeding on the way to her funeral.

1994 (2018)

The year I asked Soul Coughing to reunite to make *Ghost of Vroom* was the year before the twenty-fifth anniversary of *Ruby Vroom*.

There's not much money in a Soul Coughing reunion. Really. It'd be bigger shows than mine, but more expensive to tour; when the money's split four ways, I'd have two years of not being able to afford to go to restaurants.

It would be for the people to whom the music is meaningful.

I emailed my former bandmates and got back a hot plate of crazy.

I put a band together and toured *Ruby Vroom* myself.

1994 (2019)

Playing the album wasn't difficult. You can feel so free inside a larger piece, improvising within it. I use a structured improvisation system: hand signals, based on John Zorn's game pieces. Throw my hand out to stop the drums; break it down to a single instrument. The band as organism.

Listening to *Ruby Vroom* was difficult. I didn't want to hear who I used to be. I vibrated with shame at my tunelessness, the squeaky phrasing. My head fell in my hands.

My band laughed in disbelief; they'd been listening for twenty years. It was iconic to them.

SONGS ARE ALIVE

Songs change night by night, show by show—a word or a note drawled, clipped, pushed, elided.

I listened to old recordings just to get it right for people singing along.

For years I didn't play Soul Coughing songs. I felt liberated, but fans were shocked: those songs made them happy. After ten years, I came back to them.

Sometimes my hands on the guitar would jump automatically to the chord—like the planchette on a Ouija board: *Am I controlling this?* Sometimes it was like piloting a drone; sometimes it was like driving around an old neighborhood, *I know where to turn*, then there's an off-ramp where it's not supposed to be.

Sometimes I notice my hands; notice I'm singing the words; and I'm sucked back into my body, where do my hands go?

Sometimes I remember after excruciating seconds; sometimes I have to ask the audience.

Is this the third verse?

"Yes!" they yell. They love that.

NEW (2019)

SONGS ARE ALIVE

When I got clean, my heart was broken: heroin betrays. It stops doing what it did. You get part of the way there, but you never get there—and further from it every time you try.

I fantasized—even as life got better—that one day I could get high.

I had a conversation with an incredulous friend: if I was offered a magical deal that heroin could work for me a year and then I'd die, I'd take it.

Work at Burger King, live in an SRO. I'd take the deal. Another former dope fiend was with us. "Oh, me too, absolutely."

I dropped that fantasy. I have a more realistic one now: I'll get amnesia and forget the songs I love.

The pure-pleasure playlist, all twenty-two hours and eleven minutes of it—the experience of those songs for the first time—one after the other—hours and hours—would be better than heroin. Truly, it would be—hands down.

I did a songwriters' circle night on South Main, in Memphis. I did it like I do: three songs, shake hands, out the door. In the car, clicked the *On Repeat* playlist that Spotify puts on your feed. I hadn't checked it out; it felt like Spotify was being—obsequious?

The songs I'd discovered in recent months played, some new, some new to me: Bon Iver, "Jelmore"; DaBaby, "Baby Sitter"; Deli Girls, "Officer"; Kevin Krauter, "Pretty Boy"; Medium Medium, "Hungry, So Angry"; Junior Kimbrough, "Meet Me in the City."

Boom, boom, boom, boom.

SAINt JHN's "I Can Fvcking Tell" came on:

Girl, when the summer chills,
  you get way too dark
She stood there with her left hand on her gun, right hand
  on her heart

The world was absolutely new.

ACKNOWLEDGMENTS

A massive THANK YOU to the people whose hard work has made it possible for me to write actual real-life books and be an actual real-life writer:

Phil Frandina
Butch Gage
Paul Gutman
Jamie Kitman
Nate Meese
Frank Riley
Dave Rowan
Ben Schafer
Heather Self
Pete Smolin
Chris Tetzeli